Quick
as a wink

LEISURE ARTS, INC.
and
OXMOOR HOUSE, INC.

EDITORIAL STAFF

Vice President and Editor-in-Chief:
   Anne Van Wagner Childs
Executive Director: Sandra Graham Case
Editorial Director: Susan Frantz Wiles
Publications Director: Carla Bentley
Creative Art Director: Gloria Bearden
Senior Graphics Art Director: Melinda Stout

EDITORIAL
Managing Editor: Linda L. Trimble
Associate Editor: Darla Burdette Kelsay
Assistant Editors: Tammi Williamson Bradley,
   Terri Leming Davidson, and Robyn Sheffield-Edwards
Copy Editor: Laura Lee Weland

TECHNICAL
Managing Editor: Lisa Truxton Curton
Senior Production Coordinator:
   Connie White Irby
Production Assistant: Martha H. Carle

ART
Book/Magazine Graphics Art Director:
   Diane M. Hugo
Graphics Illustrators: Kathryn C. Goble and
   Brent Jones
Photography Stylists: Sondra Daniel, Karen Hall,
   Aurora Huston, Christina Tiano Myers,
   and Alaina Sokora

BUSINESS STAFF

Publisher: Bruce Akin
Vice President, Finance: Tom Siebenmorgen
Vice President, Retail Sales: Thomas L. Carlisle
Retail Sales Director: Richard Tignor
Vice President, Retail Marketing: Pam Stebbins
Retail Marketing Director: Margaret Sweetin
Retail Customer Services Manager: Carolyn Pruss

General Merchandise Manager: Russ Barnett
Distribution Director: Ed M. Strackbein
Vice President, Marketing: Guy A. Crossley
Marketing Manager: Byron L. Taylor
Print Production Manager: Laura Lockhart

Library of Congress Catalog Number 96-77623
Hardcover ISBN 0-8487-1561-6
Softcover ISBN 1-57486-054-2

INTRODUCTION

In no time at all, you can cross stitch delightful gifts, bright kitchen accessories, fun embellishments for clothing, and so much more! Gathered from favorite Leisure Arts publications, the versatile collections in Quick as a Wink *offer cross stitch projects that don't take a lot of time to make. You'll discover fresh new accents for your home and playful essentials for kids, as well as tailor-made presents your friends and family will love — and each item stitches up in a jiffy! We've also included projects devoted to dressing up ready-to-wear and adding feminine touches to towels, linens, and other little accessories.* Quick as a Wink *makes it a breeze to create extraordinary gifts, wearables, and decorative pieces. You'll turn to this treasure trove of speedy ideas again and again!*

TABLE

OF CONTENTS

Home Accents
IN A SNAP

It's the little touches that make a house a home — carefully chosen accents such as wreaths, towels, pillows, and portraits that reflect the unique tastes of the people who live there. The quick-to-make projects in this collection offer a variety of decorative styles, from French Country to Early American. Natural accents such as this pretty grapevine wreath add warmth and charm to your private retreat. By changing the floral heart that adorns the wreath, you can greet your guests with a Heartfelt Welcome all year long.

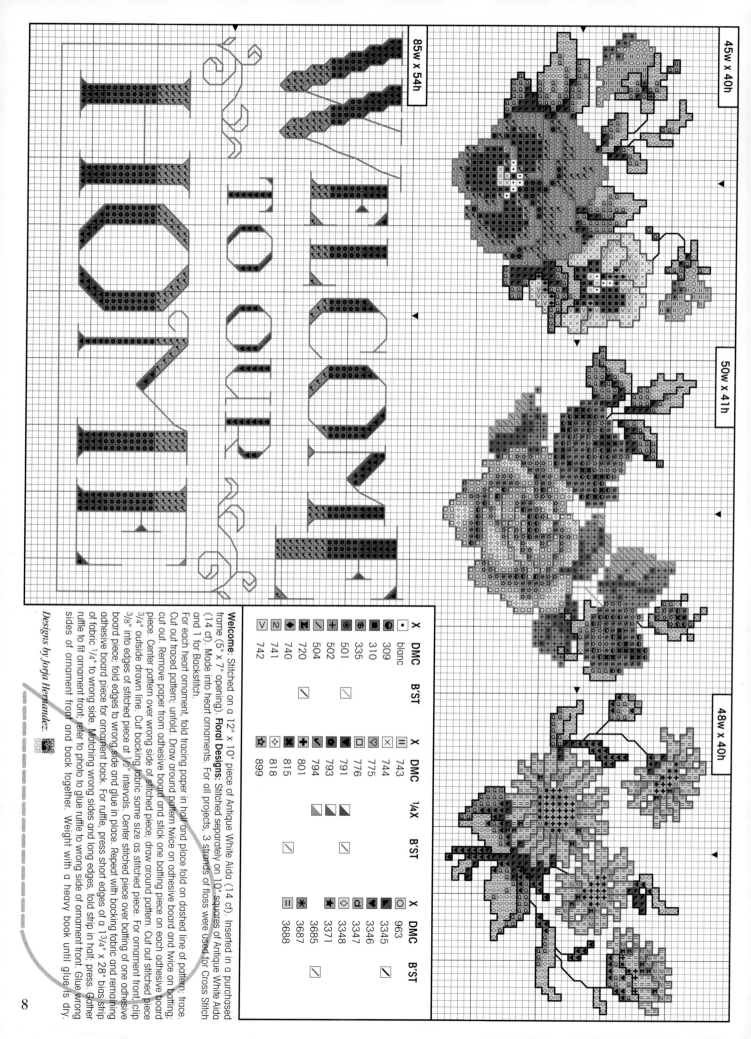

45w x 40h

50w x 41h

48w x 40h

85w x 54h

X	DMC	B'ST
•	blanc	
	309	
	310	
	335	
	501	◢
	502	
	504	
	720	◢
	740	
	741	
	742	

X	DMC	1/4X	B'ST
‖	743		
×	744		
	775		
	776	◣	
	791		
	793	◣	
	794	◣	◢
	801		
‖	815		
	818		
	899		

X	DMC	B'ST
○	963	
	3345	◹
	3346	
	3347	
	3348	
	3371	
	3685	
‖	3687	
	3688	◢

Welcome: Stitched on a 12" x 10" piece of Antique White Aida (14 ct). Inserted in a purchased frame (5" x 7" opening). Made into heart ornaments. **Floral Designs:** Stitched separately on 10" squares of Antique White Aida (14 ct). For all projects, 3 strands of floss were used for Cross Stitch and 1 for Backstitch.

For each heart ornament, fold tracing paper in half and place fold on dashed line of pattern; trace. Cut out traced pattern; unfold. Draw around pattern twice on adhesive board and twice on batting; cut out. Remove paper from adhesive board and stick one batting piece on each adhesive board piece; fold edges of stitched piece at 1/2" intervals. Cut backing fabric same size as stitched piece. For ornament front, cut 3/4" outside drawn line. Cut stitched piece at 1/2" intervals. Center stitched piece over wrong side of stitched piece; draw around pattern. Cut backing fabric same size as stitched piece. For ornament front, cut 3/4" outside drawn line. Cut stitched piece at 1/2" intervals. Center stitched piece over batting of one adhesive board piece; fold edges to wrong side and glue in place. Repeat with backing fabric and remaining adhesive board piece for ornament back. For ruffle, press short edges of a 1 3/4" x 28" bias strip of fabric 1/4" to wrong side. Matching wrong sides and long edges, fold strip in half; press. Gather ruffle to fit ornament front; refer to photo to glue ruffle to wrong side of ornament front. Glue wrong sides of ornament front and back together. Weight with a heavy book until glue is dry.

Designs by Jorja Hernandez.

LOVE GEESE

Bowing their heads together, these two affectionate geese form a heart with their graceful, curving necks. Appropriately named Love Geese, *they symbolize humble, unselfish love, making this design a beautiful wedding or anniversary gift.*

Love Geese was stitched on an 11" x 13" piece of Cream Lugana (25 ct). The design was stitched over 2 fabric threads. Three strands of floss were used for Cross Stitch, 1 for Backstitch, and 1 for French Knots. It was inserted in a purchased 5" x 7" frame.

Original artwork by Cindy Grubb, Grubbies™ *Inspirationals.*

LOVE GEESE (37w x 64h)

Aida 11	3⅜" x 5⅞"
Aida 14	2¾" x 4⅝"
Aida 18	2⅛" x 3⅝"
Hardanger 22	1¾" x 3"

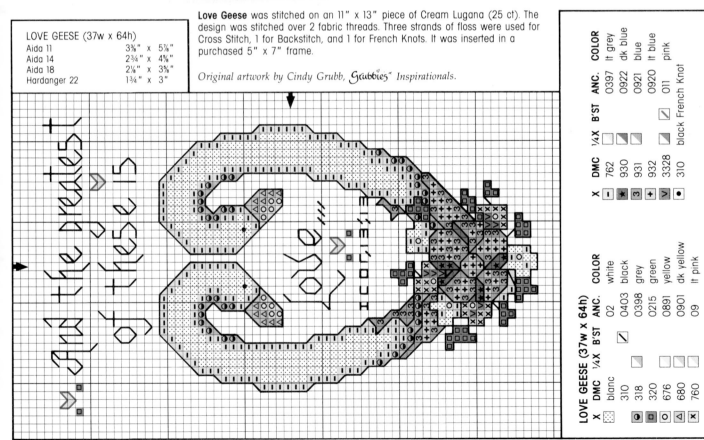

X	DMC	¼X	B'ST	ANC.	COLOR
	762			0397	lt grey
★	930			0922	dk blue
3	931			0921	blue
+	932			0920	lt blue
∨	3328			011	pink
●	310				black French Knot

X	DMC	¼X	B'ST	ANC.	COLOR
	blanc			02	white
	310			0403	black
	318			0398	grey
	320			0215	green
	676			0891	yellow
	680			0901	dk yellow
✕	760			09	lt pink

9

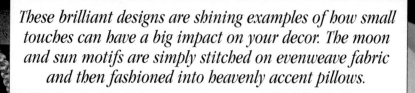

These brilliant designs are shining examples of how small touches can have a big impact on your decor. The moon and sun motifs are simply stitched on evenweave fabric and then fashioned into heavenly accent pillows.

X	DMC	¼X	B'ST	JPC	COLOR
◎	742			2303	dk yellow
✛	743			2302	yellow
⬚	745			2296	lt yellow
▬	920		╱	3337	brown
✱	922			3336	lt brown

Each design was stitched on a 10" square of Royal Blue Royal Classic (14 ct). Three strands of floss were used for Cross Stitch and 1 for Backstitch. They were each made into a pillow.

Trim stitched piece 1¾" larger than design on all sides.

For cording around stitched piece, cut one 2" x 36" bias strip of fabric. Center cording on wrong side of bias strip; matching long edges, fold strip over cord. Using zipper foot, baste along length of strip close to cord; trim seam allowance to ½". Matching raw edges and beginning at bottom edge, pin cording to right side of stitched piece, making a ⅜" clip in seam allowance of cording at each corner. Ends of cording should overlap approx. 2"; pin overlapping end out of the way. Starting 2" from beginning end of cording and ending 4" from overlapping end, sew cording to stitched piece. On overlapping end of cording, remove 2½" of basting; fold end of fabric back and trim cord so it meets beginning end of cord. Fold end of fabric under ½"; wrap fabric over beginning end of cording. Finish sewing cording to stitched piece. Press seam allowance toward stitched piece.

For pillow front and back, cut two 13" squares of fabric. Center stitched piece right side up on right side of one piece of fabric; pin in place. Using zipper foot and same color thread as cording, attach stitched piece to pillow front by sewing as close as possible to cording, taking care not to catch fabric of stitched piece.

For cording around pillow, cut one 2" x 60" bias strip of fabric. Repeat above instructions to apply cording to pillow front. Matching right sides and leaving an opening for turning, use a ½" seam allowance to sew pillow front and back together. Trim corners diagonally. Turn pillow right side out, carefully pushing corners outward. Stuff pillow with polyester fiberfill and sew final closure by hand.

Designed by Holly DeFount.

KOOLER DESIGN STUDIO

SUN (58w x 58h)

14 count	4¼"	x	4¼"
16 count	3⅝"	x	3⅝"
18 count	3¼"	x	3¼"
22 count	2¾"	x	2¾"

MOON (52w x 52h)

14 count	3¾"	x	3¾"
16 count	3¼"	x	3¼"
18 count	3"	x	3"
22 count	2⅜"	x	2⅜"

Words of comfort and an exquisite guardian angel can be beautifully framed for a friend whose loved one travels often. Our decorative jar lid and dainty fingertip towel, also stitched with celestial beings, will make sweet gifts to remind others of the loving presence that diligently watches over them.

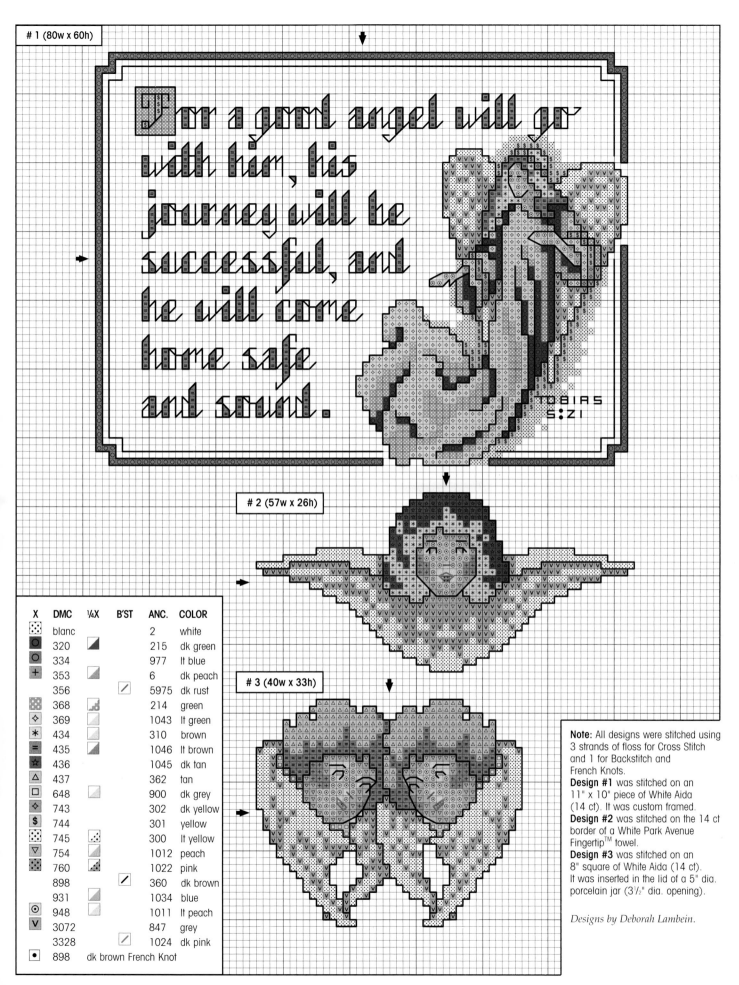

#1 (80w x 60h)

For a good angel will go with him, his journey will be successful, and he will come home safe and sound.

TOBIAS 5:21

#2 (57w x 26h)

#3 (40w x 33h)

X	DMC	¼X	B'ST	ANC.	COLOR
	blanc			2	white
	320			215	dk green
	334			977	lt blue
+	353			6	dk peach
	356		/	5975	dk rust
	368			214	green
◇	369			1043	lt green
*	434			310	brown
=	435			1046	lt brown
★	436			1045	dk tan
△	437			362	tan
□	648			900	dk grey
◆	743			302	dk yellow
$	744			301	yellow
	745			300	lt yellow
▽	754			1012	peach
	760			1022	pink
	898		/	360	dk brown
	931			1034	blue
⊙	948			1011	lt peach
V	3072			847	grey
	3328		/	1024	dk pink
•	898				dk brown French Knot

Note: All designs were stitched using 3 strands of floss for Cross Stitch and 1 for Backstitch and French Knots.
Design #1 was stitched on an 11" x 10" piece of White Aida (14 ct). It was custom framed.
Design #2 was stitched on the 14 ct border of a White Park Avenue Fingertip™ towel.
Design #3 was stitched on an 8" square of White Aida (14 ct). It was inserted in the lid of a 5" dia. porcelain jar (3½" dia. opening).

Designs by Deborah Lambein.

13

DUCKS
OF THE
WILD

These impressive ducks were adapted from the wildlife prints of Alice Taylor, one of America's foremost sporting artists. Stitched individually or as a set with a coordinating box, the designs make a handsome display in an office or study.

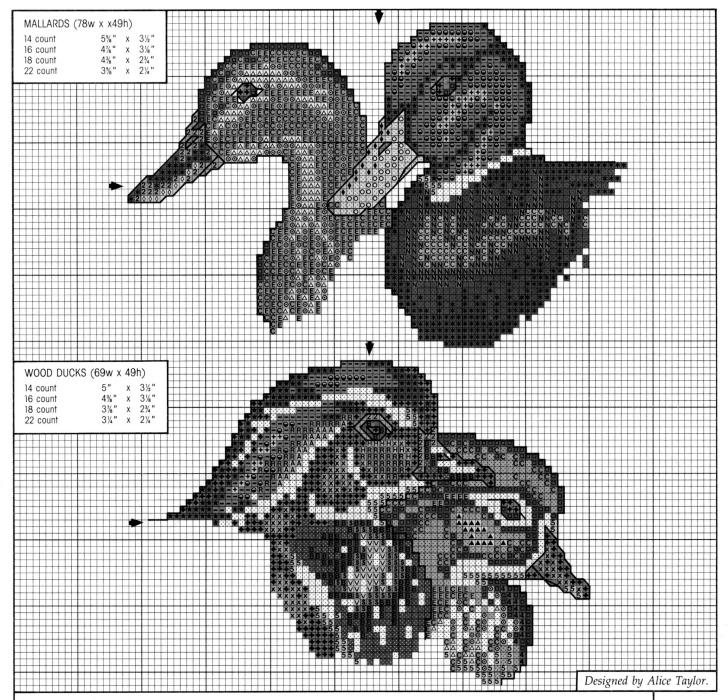

MALLARDS (78w x x49h)

14 count	5⅝"	x 3½"
16 count	4⅞"	x 3⅛"
18 count	4⅜"	x 2¾"
22 count	3⅝"	x 2¼"

WOOD DUCKS (69w x 49h)

14 count	5"	x 3½"
16 count	4⅜"	x 3⅛"
18 count	3⅞"	x 2¾"
22 count	3¼"	x 2¼"

Designed by Alice Taylor.

MALLARDS (78w x 49h)
WOOD DUCKS (69w x 49h)

X	DMC	¼X	B'ST	JPC	COLOR
	blanc			1001	white
	221			3242	vy dk rust
◆	310		/	8403	black
R	315			3082	mauve
A	316			3081	lt mauve
S	355			2339	rust
V	356			2975	lt rust
5	415			8398	grey
⊙	437			5942	tan
2	720			2322	orange
◊	721			2324	lt orange
O	725			2298	lt gold
△	739			5369	cream
◆	781			5309	dk gold

X	DMC	¼X	B'ST	JPC	COLOR
	783			5307	gold
4	839			5360	dk beige
	840			5379	beige
E	841			5578	lt beige
▲	842			5933	vy lt beige
★	890			6021	vy dk green
−	895			6021	dk green
✳	918			3340	vy dk copper
	919			2326	dk copper
N	920			3337	copper
C	921				lt copper
⊖	986			6021	green
+	987			6258	lt green
□	3031			5472	brown

X	DMC	¼X	B'ST	JPC	COLOR
H	3740				violet
B	3777				dk rust
C	3781				lt brown
X	3799			8999	steel grey
⊙	blanc		white French Knot		

Mallards: Stitched over 2 fabric threads on a 14" x 12" piece of Tea-Dyed Irish Linen (28 ct). Two strands of floss used for Cross Stitch and 1 for all other stitches. Custom framed.

Wood Ducks: Stitched over 2 fabric threads on a 13" x 12" piece of Tea-Dyed Irish Linen (28 ct). Two strands of floss used for Cross Stitch and 1 for all other stitches. Custom framed.

Male Wood Duck **only** stitched over 2 fabric threads on a 12" x 12" piece of Tea-Dyed Irish Linen (28 ct). Two strands of floss used for Cross Stitch and 1 for all other stitches. Inserted in a purchased wooden box (5" dia. opening).

15

Amish quilts are some of the most wonderful examples of
our country's rich needlework heritage. Out of admiration for
these people and their talents, we created these cross-stitched
miniature versions of their bold and beautiful patterns.

(45w x 45h)

(57w x 57h)

(43w x 43h)

(53w x 53h)

MINI AMISH QUILTS

X	DMC	ANC.	COLOR	X	DMC	ANC.	COLOR
S	333	0119	violet	X	943	0188	aqua
♦	817	047	red	∕	Indicates quilting lines.		
O	909	0229	green				

Note: When stitching on dark evenweave fabric, place a piece of white paper or fabric on your lap. The holes of the fabric will be easier to see when held over a white surface. It may be necessary to increase number of floss strands to ensure good coverage of fabric.

The **Mini Amish Quilts** were stitched on 7" x 7" pieces of Black Lugana (25 ct). The designs were stitched over 2 threads. Three strands of floss were used for Cross Stitch. They were made into mini quilts.

For each mini quilt, cut stitched piece ¾" larger than design on all sides. Cut backing fabric and batting same size as stitched piece.

Center batting on wrong side of stitched piece and baste together ⅛" from edges. With right sides facing and matching raw edges, use a ¼" seam allowance to sew stitched piece and backing fabric together, leaving an opening at bottom edge. Trim batting in seam allowance close to stitching. Clip seam allowances at corners. Turn right side out, carefully pushing corners outward. Fold edges of opening ¼" to inside; whipstitch opening closed.

Use quilting thread and refer to black lines on chart to quilt around designs; then quilt around entire mini quilt ¼" from edges.

Quilting Stitch

Knot one end of quilting thread. Bring needle up through all layers of quilt; pop knot through fabric into batting.

To quilt, stitch through all layers and use small running stitches that are equal in length (**Fig. 1**).

At the end of a length of thread, knot thread and take needle down through quilt; pop knot through fabric into batting. Clip thread close to fabric.

Fig. 1

A TIMELY CLOCK

Featuring a colorful cornucopia, this classic carriage clock offers a timely way to celebrate life's bounty.

Clock: Stitched on an 11" x 13" piece of Ivory Aida (18 ct). Two strands of floss used for Cross Stitch, 2 for vy dk olive Backstitch numbers, 2 for dk tan Backstitch border, and 1 strand for all other Backstitch. Inserted in a purchased clock.

Designed by Donna Vermillion Giampa.

CLOCK (55w x 81h)

X	DMC	1/4X	B'ST	JPC	COLOR
	209			4302	purple
	211			4303	lt purple
	350			3111	dk salmon
	352			3008	salmon
	368			6016	lt green
	498			3410	red
	611			5898	dk beige
	612				beige
	613				lt beige

X	DMC	1/4X	B'ST	JPC	COLOR
	666			3046	lt red
	740			2099	lt orange
	742			2303	yellow
	869				dk tan
	900			2329	vy dk tan
	919			2326	dk orange
	935			6270	rust
	947			2327	orange
	986			6021	dk green

X	DMC	1/4X	B'ST	JPC	COLOR
	988			6258	green
	3011			6845	dk olive
	3012			6843	olive
	3013			6842	lt olive
	3021			5395	vy dk beige
	3045			2412	dk tan
	3046			2410	tan
	3047				lt tan
	3746			2300	dk purple

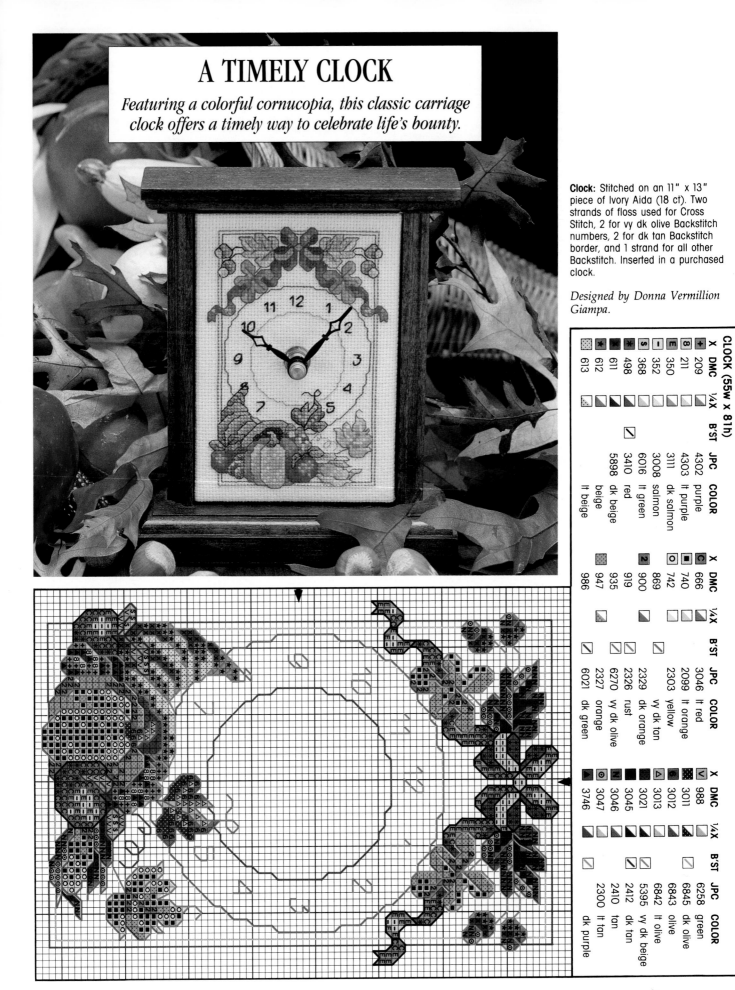

AMERICAN TEDDY

Everyone wants to show off his American pride during the spirited festivities of the Fourth of July. Posed against a field of stars and stripes, this little patriot bear is all decked out for the celebration.

American Teddy was stitched on an 8" x 9" piece of Ivory Aida (14 ct). Three strands of floss were used for Cross Stitch and 1 for Half Cross Stitch and Backstitch. It was inserted in a purchased frame (4" x 6" opening).

Original artwork by Debra Jordan Meyer. Needlework adaptation by Jane Chandler.

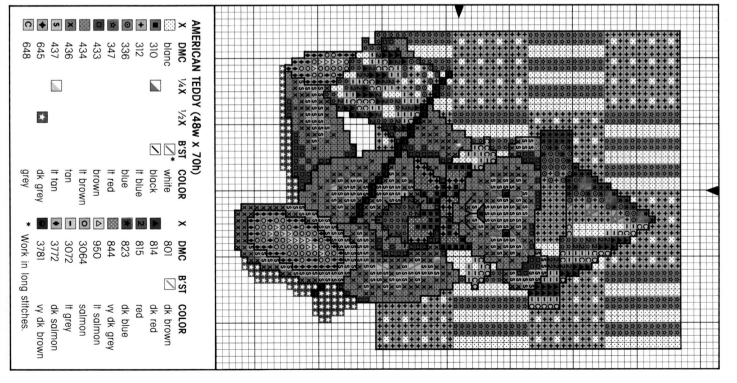

AMERICAN TEDDY (48w x 70h)

X	DMC	1/4X	1/2X	B'ST	COLOR	X	DMC	B'ST	COLOR
	blanc				white		801		dk brown
	310			*	black		814		dk red
	312	◹			lt blue		815		red
	336				blue		823	◹	dk blue
	347				lt red		844		vy dk grey
	433				brown		950		lt salmon
	434				lt brown		3064		salmon
	436				tan		3072		lt grey
	437		★		lt tan		3772		dk salmon
	645				dk grey		3781		vy dk brown
	648				grey				

* Work in long stitches.

These old-fashioned mini samplers capture
the charm of yesteryear's needlework.
Personalized with your initials and finished
in purchased frames, the quick-to-stitch
designs make sweet friendship tokens as well
as quaint pieces for your home.

Designed by Deborah Payne Baker.

OLD-TIME MINI SAMPLERS

X	DMC	SATIN STITCH	B'ST	JPC	COLOR
◐	315		✓	3082	mauve
+	316			3081	lt mauve
◇	680		✓	2876	gold
−	761			3068	rose
✳	924		✓	6008	blue
C	926	✓		6007	lt blue
★	3051		✓	6317	green

Note: For projects, 3 strands of floss were used for Cross Stitch, 3 for Satin Stitch, and 1 for Backstitch. They were inserted in purchased frames (4" x 5" opening).

Design #1 was stitched over 2 fabric threads on a 7" x 8" piece of Tea-Dyed Irish Linen (28 ct). The date and initials were stitched using DMC 931.

Design #2 was stitched over 2 fabric threads on a 7" x 9" piece of Tea-Dyed Irish Linen (28 ct). The date and initials were stitched using DMC 924.

Design #3 was stitched over 2 fabric threads on an 8" square of Tea-Dyed Irish Linen (28 ct). The date and initials were stitched using DMC 924.

STITCH DIAGRAM

Satin Stitch: For Satin Stitches, follow **Fig. 1** to come up at odd numbers and go down at even numbers.

Fig. 1

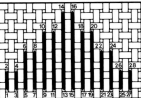

Black fabric provides a dramatic background for this stately eagle, a proud symbol of our American heritage. The regal bird makes a fitting accent for your home on patriotic holidays — or let your national spirit shine by displaying it all year through.

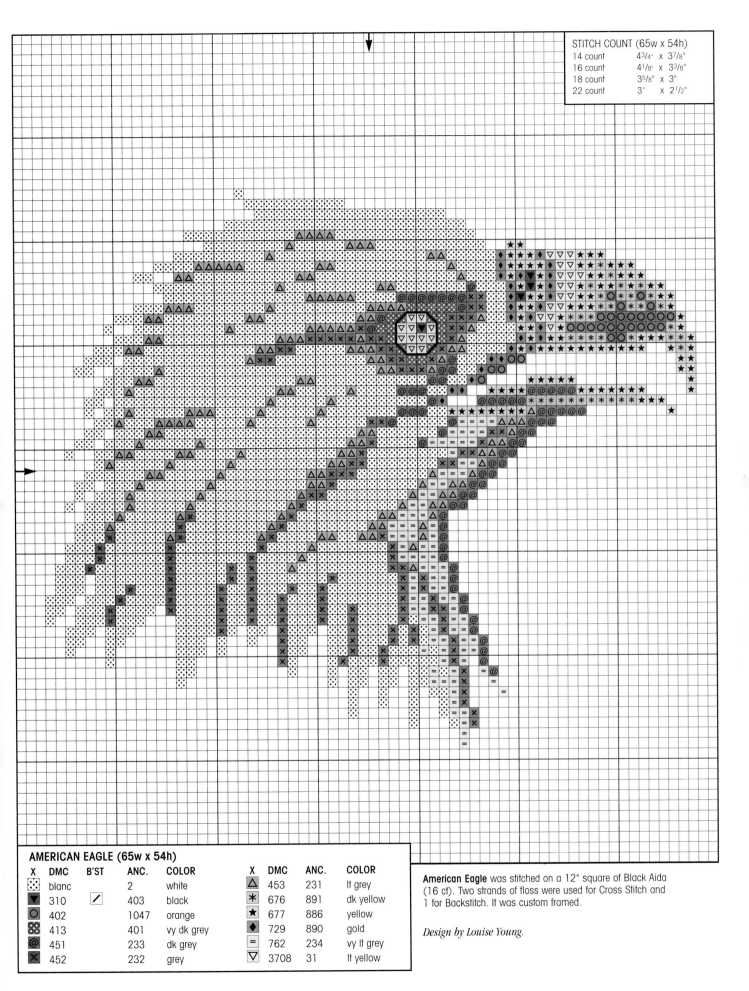

STITCH COUNT (65w x 54h)

14 count	4³/₄"	x 3⁷/₈"
16 count	4¹/₈"	x 3³/₈"
18 count	3⁵/₈"	x 3"
22 count	3"	x 2¹/₂"

AMERICAN EAGLE (65w x 54h)

X	DMC	B'ST	ANC.	COLOR
blanc			2	white
310		✓	403	black
402			1047	orange
413			401	vy dk grey
451			233	dk grey
452			232	grey

X	DMC	ANC.	COLOR
453		231	lt grey
676		891	dk yellow
677		886	yellow
729		890	gold
762		234	vy lt grey
3708		31	lt yellow

American Eagle was stitched on a 12" square of Black Aida (16 ct). Two strands of floss were used for Cross Stitch and 1 for Backstitch. It was custom framed.

Design by Louise Young.

23

Stitched on prefinished hand towels, these classic seashell designs will give your bath the look of a seaside retreat. The handsome shells will make your guests feel like they're on an island vacation!

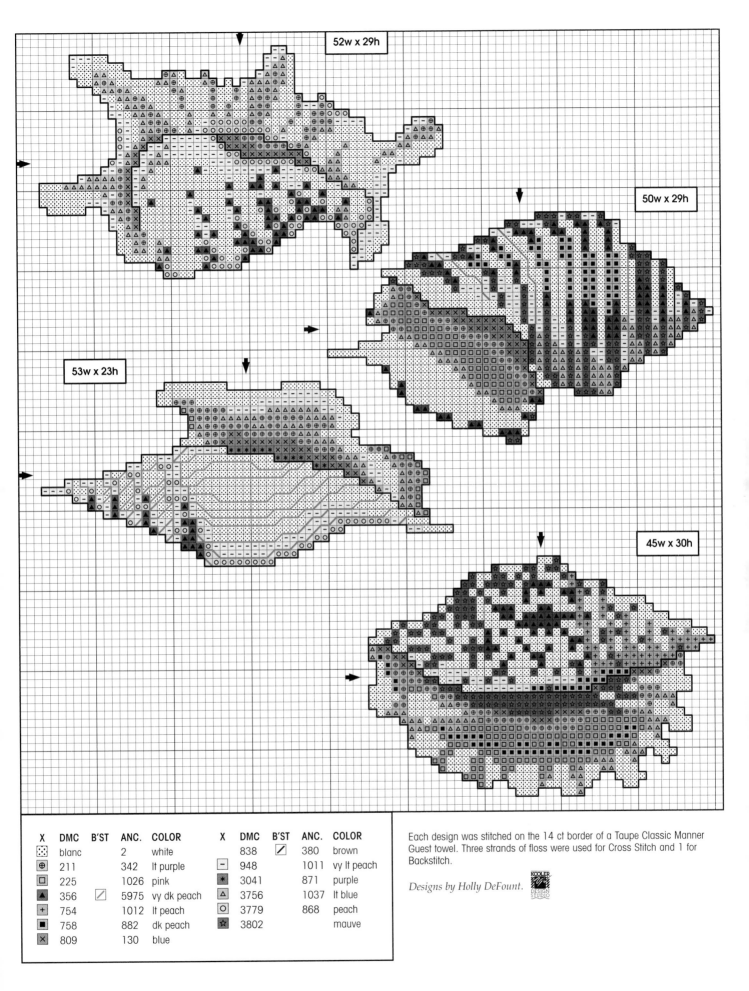

X	DMC	B'ST	ANC.	COLOR	X	DMC	B'ST	ANC.	COLOR
▨	blanc		2	white		838	╱	380	brown
⊕	211		342	lt purple	–	948		1011	vy lt peach
◻	225		1026	pink	✳	3041		871	purple
▲	356	╱	5975	vy dk peach	△	3756		1037	lt blue
+	754		1012	lt peach	○	3779		868	peach
▪	758		882	dk peach	☆	3802			mauve
✕	809		130	blue					

Each design was stitched on the 14 ct border of a Taupe Classic Manner Guest towel. Three strands of floss were used for Cross Stitch and 1 for Backstitch.

Designs by Holly DeFount.

KOOLER DESIGN STUDIO

A Dash
OF FEMININITY

Pretty bouquets of flowers scattered throughout the house hint at romance and set an inviting mood. The soft, feminine floral designs in this collection let you indulge yourself in beauty every day. Lavish them on towels, linens, and other little accessories to create a gardenful of blooms. Beautifully preserved in cross stitch, these Picture-Perfect Roses *capture the gracefulness of one of our most beloved flowers.*

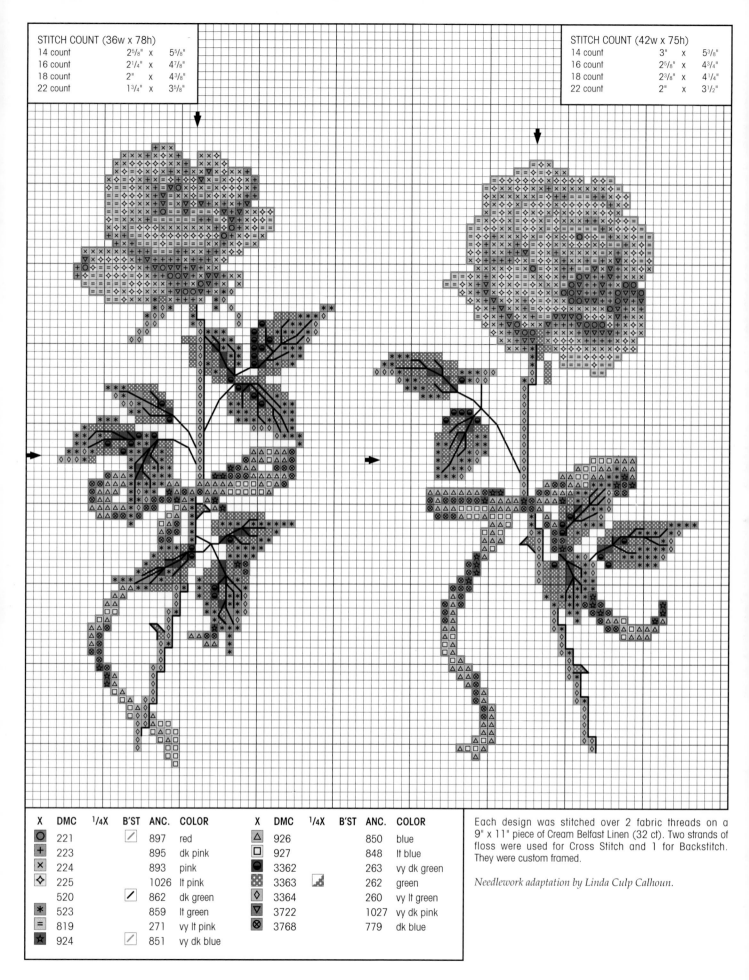

X	DMC	¼X	B'ST	ANC.	COLOR		X	DMC	¼X	B'ST	ANC.	COLOR
⊙	221		╱	897	red		△	926			850	blue
+	223			895	dk pink		◻	927			848	lt blue
×	224			893	pink		◑	3362			263	vy dk green
◆	225			1026	lt pink		▨	3363		◢	262	green
	520		╱	862	dk green		◇	3364			260	vy lt green
✳	523			859	lt green		▽	3722			1027	vy dk pink
=	819			271	vy lt pink		⊗	3768			779	dk blue
★	924		╱	851	vy dk blue							

Each design was stitched over 2 fabric threads on a 9" x 11" piece of Cream Belfast Linen (32 ct). Two strands of floss were used for Cross Stitch and 1 for Backstitch. They were custom framed.

Needlework adaptation by Linda Culp Calhoun.

DELICATE DRESSER SCARF

Splendid roses and tiny blue blossoms embellish each end of our linen scarf, a quick-to-make accessory that will add instant charm to a table or dresser.

105w x 35h

The design was stitched across each end of a 13¹⁄₂" x 36" piece of Cream Bantry Cloth (28 ct) with bottom edge of design 1³⁄₄" from short edge of fabric. The design was stitched over 2 fabric threads. Three strands of floss were used for Cross Stitch and 1 for Backstitch.

For dresser scarf, cut two 14" lengths of 1"w flat lace. Press each short edge of lace ¹⁄₄" to wrong side. Match right sides and align straight edge of one length of lace with one short raw edge of stitched piece. Using a ¹⁄₄" seam allowance, sew both layers together. Using a zigzag stitch, sew over raw edges to prevent fraying. Press seam allowance toward stitched piece. Repeat with remaining short edge of stitched piece and length of lace.

Design by Jorja Hernandez for Kooler Design Studio.

X	DMC	B'ST	ANC.	COLOR	X	DMC	B'ST	ANC.	COLOR
	311	∕	148	vy dk blue	V	368		214	vy lt green
◆	319		218	dk green	−	725		305	yellow
C	320		215	lt green	O	760		1022	lt pink
◓	322		978	dk blue	+	761		1021	vy lt pink
◻	334		977	blue		890	∕	218	dk green
▲	347		1025	dk pink	☆	3328		1024	pink
	355	∕	1014	vy dk pink	✕	3755		140	lt blue
2	367		217	green					

29

With their delicate flowers and sweet hearts, our trio of bread covers will invite spring to linger at your table. These simple designs are ideal for the stitcher who enjoys quick-to-finish projects.

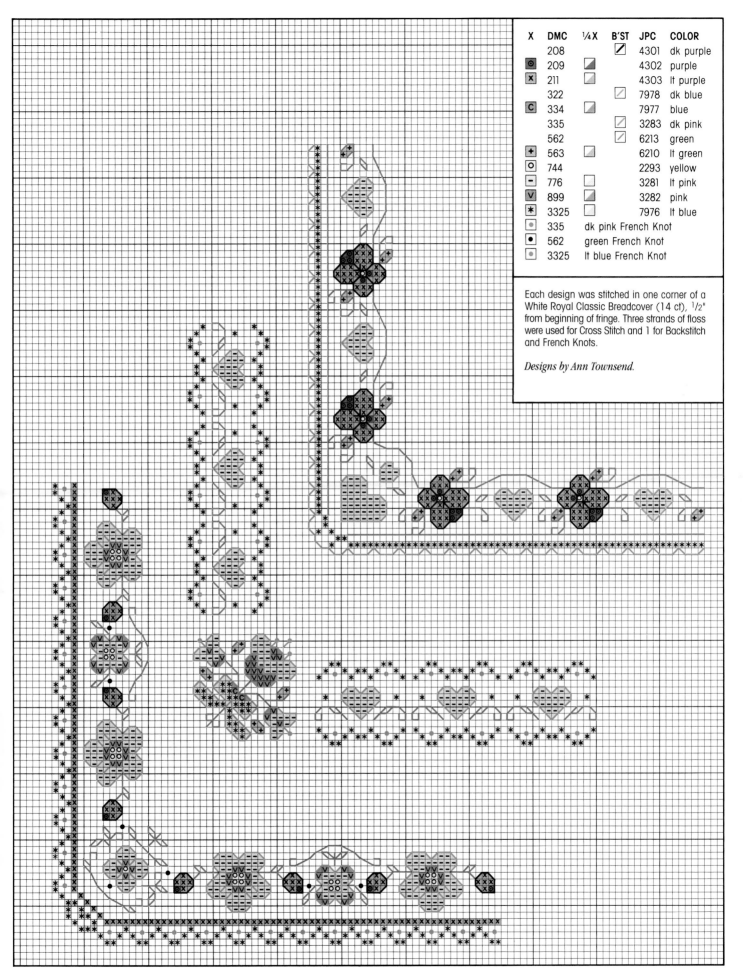

X	DMC	¼X	B'ST	JPC	COLOR
	208		╱	4301	dk purple
⊙	209	◩		4302	purple
✗	211	◩		4303	lt purple
	322		╱	7978	dk blue
C	334	◩		7977	blue
	335		╱	3283	dk pink
	562		╱	6213	green
+	563	◩		6210	lt green
O	744			2293	yellow
−	776	◻		3281	lt pink
V	899	◩		3282	pink
✲	3325	◻		7976	lt blue
◦	335		dk pink French Knot		
●	562		green French Knot		
◦	3325		lt blue French Knot		

Each design was stitched in one corner of a White Royal Classic Breadcover (14 ct), ½" from beginning of fringe. Three strands of floss were used for Cross Stitch and 1 for Backstitch and French Knots.

Designs by Ann Townsend.

ROMANTIC MONOGRAMS

*Pretty little accessories for your boudoir become treasured
heirlooms when monogrammed with our hearts and flowers alphabet.
The tiny keepsakes make beautiful gifts for loved ones, too.*

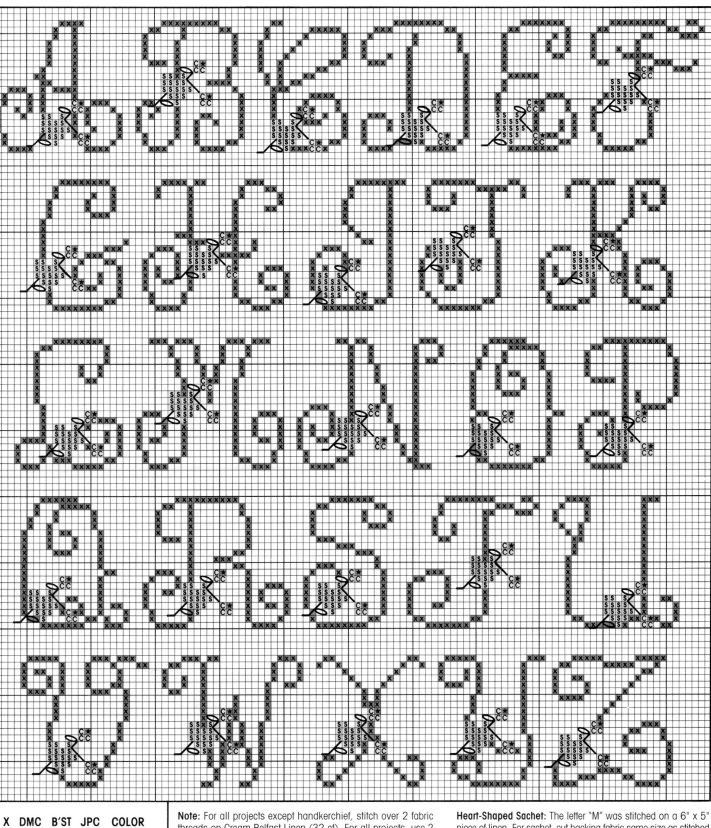

X	DMC	B'ST	JPC	COLOR
S	223		3241	pink
	501	✓	6878	green
×	640		5393	brown
★	930		7052	blue
C	931		7051	lt blue
∅	501			green Lazy Daisy Stitch

Note: For all projects except handkerchief, stitch over 2 fabric threads on Cream Belfast Linen (32 ct). For all projects, use 2 strands of floss for Cross Stitch and 1 for all other stitches.
Handkerchief: The letter "H" was stitched over a 2¹/2" x 2¹/2" piece of waste canvas (18 ct) in the corner of an 11" square of cotton fabric (see Working on Waste Canvas, page 143). For handkerchief, refer to photo for placement and stitch letter. Fold each edge of fabric ¹/4" to wrong side; press. Fold ¹/4" again; hem. Sew desired pregathered lace trim to edges of handkerchief.

Heart-Shaped Sachet: The letter "M" was stitched on a 6" x 5" piece of linen. For sachet, cut backing fabric same size as stitched piece. Trace heart pattern (see page 144) onto tracing paper; cut out pattern.
With right sides facing and matching raw edges, place stitched piece and backing fabric together. Center pattern on wrong side of stitched piece. Use fabric marking pencil to draw around pattern. Cut out fabric pieces.
Continued on page 144.

Trimmed with lace, our delicate cross-stitched towels will add a timeless touch to your home. They'll also make tasteful gifts for friends who share your love of old-fashioned elegance.

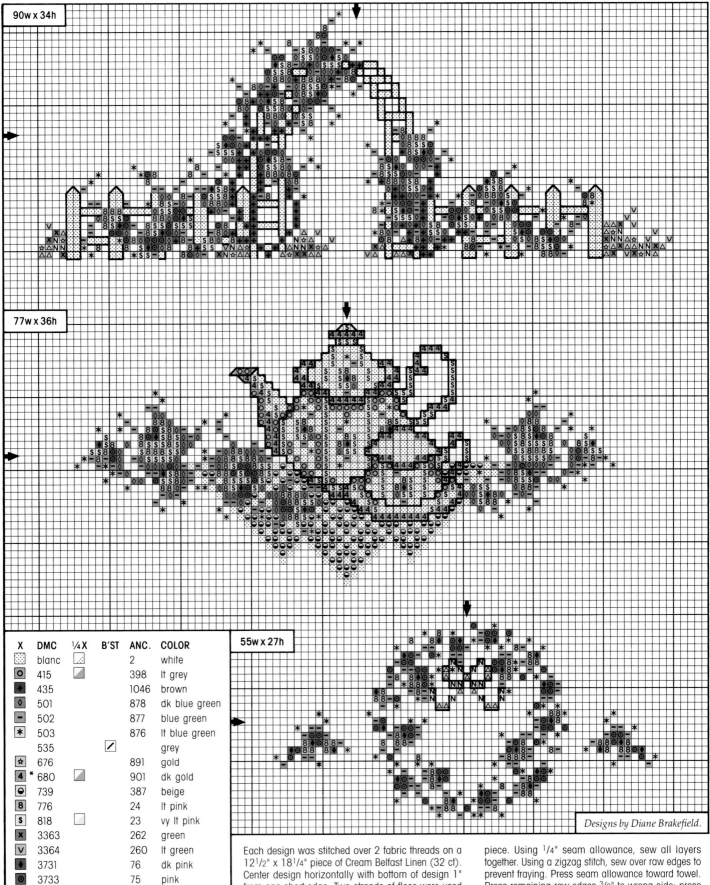

90w x 34h

77w x 36h

55w x 27h

X	DMC	¼X	B'ST	ANC.	COLOR
⠿	blanc	⠿		2	white
◉	415	◢		398	lt grey
✳	435			1046	brown
◈	501			878	dk blue green
−	502			877	blue green
✲	503			876	lt blue green
	535		╱		grey
☆	676			891	gold
4 *	680	◢		901	dk gold
⊖	739			387	beige
8	776			24	lt pink
S	818	◱		23	vy lt pink
X	3363			262	green
V	3364			260	lt green
◆	3731			76	dk pink
◉	3733			75	pink
N	3761			928	lt blue
△	3766			167	blue

* Use 1 strand of floss and 2 strands
   of Kreinik Blending Filament - 002.

Designs by Diane Brakefield.

Each design was stitched over 2 fabric threads on a 12½" x 18¼" piece of Cream Belfast Linen (32 ct). Center design horizontally with bottom of design 1" from one short edge. Two strands of floss were used for Cross Stitch and 1 for Backstitch. They were made into towels.

For each towel, cut one 12½" length of 1¼"w flat lace. On cross-stitched end, match right sides and align straight end of lace with short raw edge of stitched piece. Using ¼" seam allowance, sew all layers together. Using a zigzag stitch, sew over raw edges to prevent fraying. Press seam allowance toward towel. Press remaining raw edges ³⁄₈" to wrong side; press ³⁄₈" to wrong side again and hem.

Pretty and petite, our floral borders make lovely accents for sachets. Shared with someone special, the fragrant bags are sweet tokens of friendship.

Each design was stitched on a White Aida (14 ct) prefinished sachet bag with bottom of design placed 1″ from bottom of bag. Three strands of floss were used for Cross Stitch and 1 for all other stitches. Refer to photo to repeat designs.

Designed by Ann Townsend.

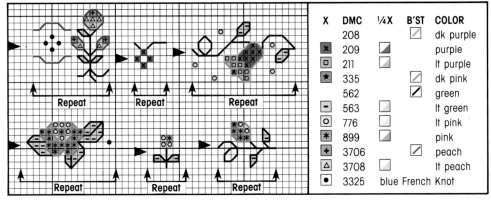

X	DMC	¼X	B'ST	COLOR
	208		/	dk purple
X	209	◧		purple
▢	211	◧		lt purple
★	335		/	dk pink
	562		/	green
−	563	◧		lt green
○	776	◧		lt pink
*	899	◧		pink
+	3706		/	peach
△	3708	◧		lt peach
●	3325			blue French Knot

Repeat

36

A friend will delight in the glory of summer with these fingertip towels. Illustrating three favorite sights of the season, the softly colored designs will make a nice addition to her bath.

X	¼X	B'ST	DMC	COLOR
●			301	dk orange
●			340	lavender
◇			413	grey
◇		◪	552	dk purple
◉			553	purple
★	◪◪◪		554	lt purple
✕			562	dk green
▶			563	green
☆			743	dk yellow
▷	◪		745	yellow
■	◪		745	lt yellow
S		◪	813	blue
I	◪◪		826	dk blue
C			937	dk yellow green
+			964	turquoise
✱			977	orange
◆	◪		3346	yellow green
2			3347	lt yellow green
			3608	dk pink
◖			3609	pink
			3747	lt lavender
			3766	lt blue
			301	dk orange French Knot
			413	grey French Knot

Each design was stitched on the White Aida (14 ct) insert of a fingertip towel. Three strands of floss were used for Cross Stitch and 1 for all other stitches.

Designed by Jorja Hernandez for Kooler Design Studio.

43w x 18h

38w x 21h

45w x 21h

Give a gift of springtime cheer with any one or all four of our lacy fingertip towels stitched with flower borders.

X	DMC	¼X	B'ST	ANC.	COLOR
▨	208	▧	▨	110	purple
✚	211	▧		342	lt purple
◈	322	▧		978	blue
	335	▧		38	dk pink
	562	▧		210	green

X	DMC	¼X	ANC.	COLOR
▬	563	▧	208	lt green
✳	744		301	yellow
C	776		24	lt pink
✿	899		55	pink
△	3325	▧	144	lt blue

X	DMC	COLOR
•	208	purple French Knot
•	335	dk pink French Knot
•	3325	lt blue French Knot

Each design was stitched on the White Aida (14ct) panel of a velour fingertip towel. Three strands of floss were used for Cross Stitch and 1 for Backstitch and French Knots.

Designed by Ann Townsend.

39

These soft floral designs welcome spring on a variety of home accessories.

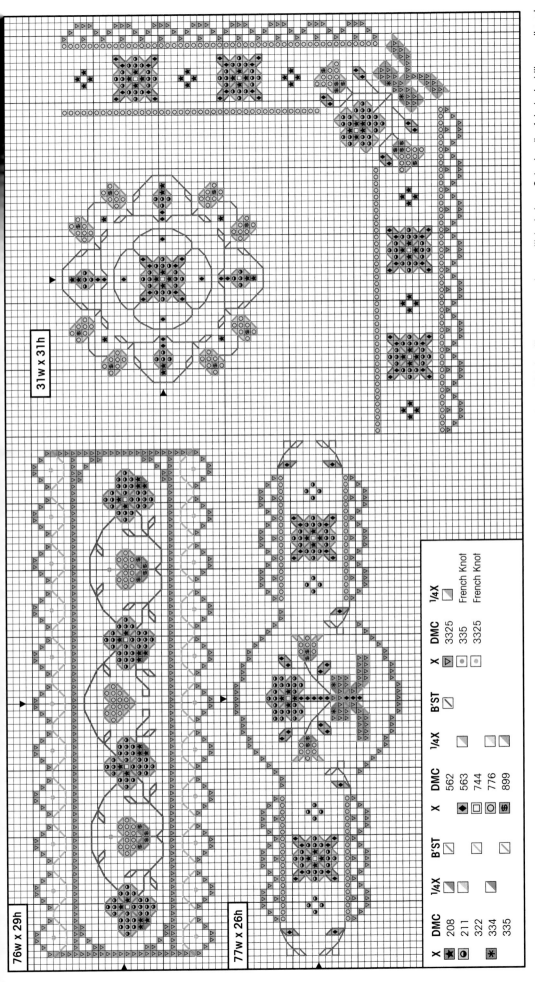

76w x 29h

31w x 31h

77w x 26h

X	DMC	1/4X	B'ST
★	208		
◑	211		
	322		
	334		
✱	335		

X	DMC	1/4X	B'ST
	562		
◆	563		
□	744		
○	776		
$	899		

X	DMC	1/4X	
▷	3325		
○	335		French Knot
□	3325		French Knot

All projects other than Towel were stitched on White Belfast Linen (32 ct) over 2 fabric threads. For all projects, 3 strands of floss were used for Cross Stitch and 1 for all other stitches.

Basket Cloth: Stitch design in one corner of a 19" square of fabric with outermost edges of design 1 1/2" from edges of fabric. Press edges of fabric 1/4" to wrong side; press 1/4" to wrong side again and hem. Cut a 2 1/4 yd length of desired width pregathered lace; press short edges 1/2" to wrong side. Refer to photo to whipstitch gathered edge of lace along edges of cloth. Join pressed edges of lace using blind stitches.

Candle Ring: Center and stitch design; trim stitched piece to desired size plus 1/2" on all sides. Press long edges 1/2" to wrong side. Cut a length of desired width pregathered lace the length of long edge of stitched piece. Refer to photo to whipstitch gathered edge of lace to wrong side of stitched piece along bottom edge. Press short edges 1/2" to wrong side. Place Candle Ring around candle and whipstitch short edges together.

Sachet Bag: Center and stitch design on a 4" x 6" piece of fabric with bottom of design 1 1/2" from one short edge. Cut backing fabric (same fabric as stitched piece) same size as stitched piece. Matching right sides and raw edges, use a 1/2" seam allowance to sew stitched piece and backing fabric together along bottom and side edges. Trim bottom corner seam allowances diagonally. Press top edge of bag 1/4" to wrong side; press 1/4" to wrong side again and hem. Cut a 7" length of desired width pregathered lace; press short edges 1/2" to wrong side. Refer to photo to whipstitch gathered edge of lace along top edge of bag. Join pressed edges of lace using blind stitches. Turn bag right side out. Stuff bag with polyester fiberfill. Place a few drops of scented oil on a small amount of fiberfill and insert in middle of bag. Tie two 15" lengths of 1/16"w ribbon in a bow around bag; trim ends as desired.

Sachet Pillow: Center and stitch design; trim stitched piece to desired size plus 1/2" on all sides. Cut backing fabric (same fabric as stitched piece) same size as stitched piece. Cut a length of desired width pregathered lace the outer dimension of pillow top plus 1"; press short edges 1/2" to wrong side. Matching right sides and starting at bottom edge of pillow top, use a 1/2" seam allowance to sew lace to pillow top with finished edge toward center of pillow top and gathered edge facing outward. Join pressed edges of lace using blind stitches. Matching right sides and raw edges, use a 1/2" seam allowance to sew pillow top and backing fabric together, leaving an opening at bottom edge. Trim corner seam allowances diagonally. Turn pillow right side out, carefully pushing corners outward. Stuff pillow with polyester fiberfill. Place a few drops of scented oil on a small amount of fiberfill and insert in middle of pillow. Sew final closure by hand.

Towel: Center and stitch design on a White Linen Additions™ (28 ct) over 2 fabric threads; refer to photo to whipstitch Additions™ to a hand towel.

Designs by Ann Townsend.

Little Folks' EXPRESS

Exciting colors and designs mark this collection of playful essentials for babies and children. The quick-and-easy projects will get your little ones off to a smart start — and there are several designs that will grow with them. You'll find lots of bibs and a bottle warmer for baby, plus an afghan, towels, and an assortment of jar lids and bookmarks for older children. These Heartwarming Bibs are guaranteed to put a twinkle in the proud parents' eyes — and get lots of attention for baby, too!

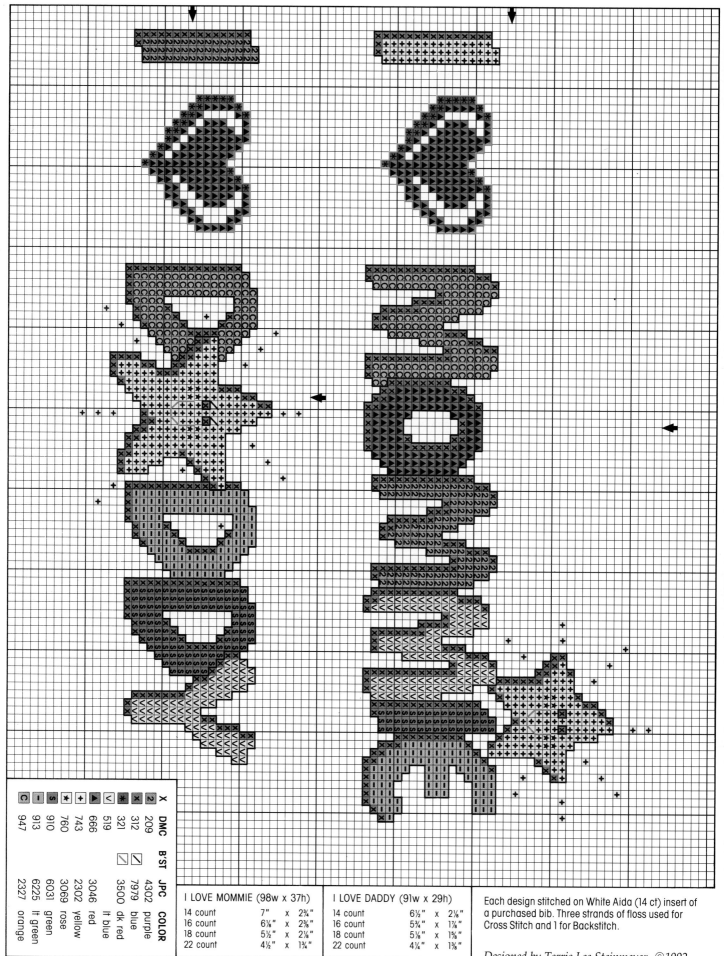

C	I	S	★	+	▶	V	✳	✕	2	X					
DMC	209	312	321	519	666	743	760	910	913	947			**B'ST**		
													╲	╱	
JPC	4302	7979	3500	3410	3046	2302	3069	6031	6225	2327					
COLOR	purple	blue	dk red	lt blue	red	yellow	rose	green	lt green	orange					

I LOVE MOMMIE (98w x 37h)			I LOVE DADDY (91w x 29h)			Each design stitched on White Aida (14 ct) insert of a purchased bib. Three strands of floss used for Cross Stitch and 1 for Backstitch.
14 count	7"	x 2¾"	14 count	6½"	x 2⅛"	
16 count	6⅛"	x 2⅜"	16 count	5¾"	x 1⅞"	
18 count	5½"	x 2⅛"	18 count	5⅛"	x 1⅝"	
22 count	4½"	x 1¾"	22 count	4¼"	x 1⅜"	

Designed by Terrie Lee Steinmeyer, ©1992.

MOO BABIES

Our bovine baby accessories are simply divine! Sporting cute cows, the matching bib and sipper cup will make mealtime "a-moo-singly" fun for your little one.

Design #1 was centered and stitched on a 7½" x 3" piece of Vinyl-Weave™ (14 ct). Three strands of floss were used for Cross Stitch and 1 for Backstitch. It was inserted in a Stitch-A-Sipper™. Hand wash to protect stitchery.

Design #2 was centered and stitched on the White Aida (14 ct) insert of a purchased baby bib. Three strands of floss were used for Cross Stitch and 1 for Backstitch.

Designed by Terrie Lee Steinmeyer. ©1994

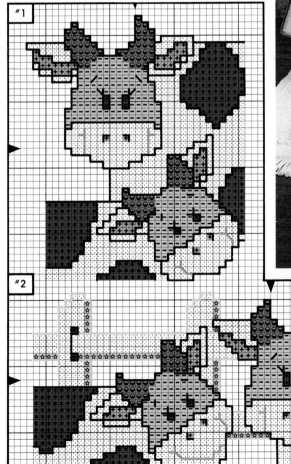

CUTE COWS				
X	DMC	B'ST	ANC.	COLOR
	blanc		2	white
	335	/	38	dk pink
	413	/	401	dk grey
◕	436		1045	dk tan
-	738		361	tan
☆	762		234	grey
+	776		24	pink
✳	898	/	360	brown

These fun-filled party jars are wonderful treats to make for a child's birthday bash.

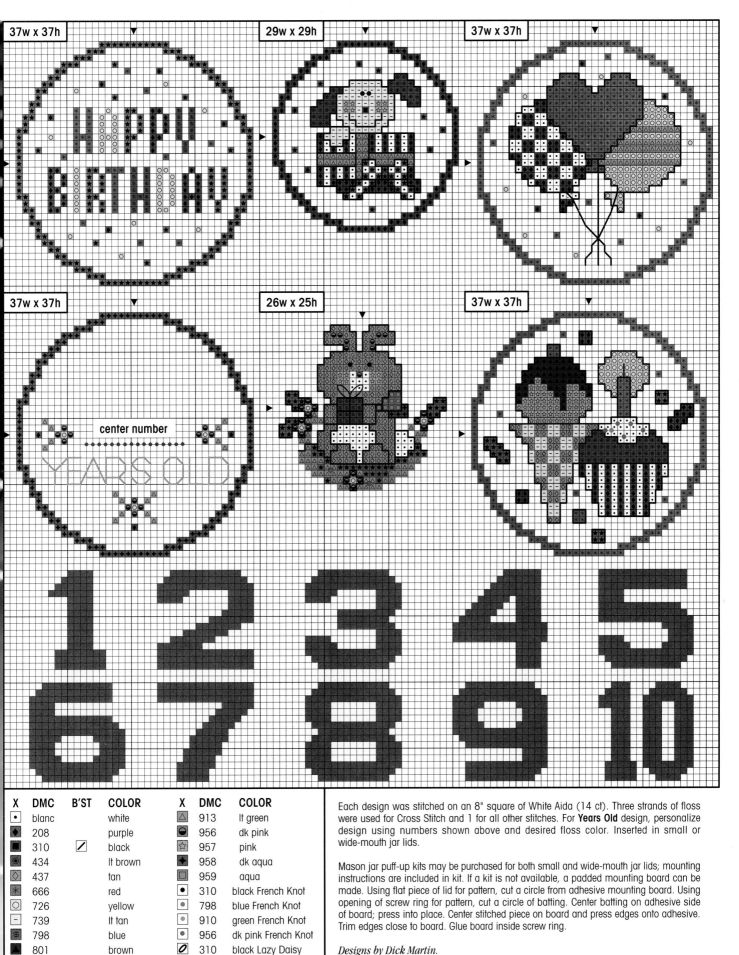

Each design was stitched on an 8" square of White Aida (14 ct). Three strands of floss were used for Cross Stitch and 1 for all other stitches. For **Years Old** design, personalize design using numbers shown above and desired floss color. Inserted in small or wide-mouth jar lids.

Mason jar puff-up kits may be purchased for both small and wide-mouth jar lids; mounting instructions are included in kit. If a kit is not available, a padded mounting board can be made. Using flat piece of lid for pattern, cut a circle from adhesive mounting board. Using opening of screw ring for pattern, cut a circle of batting. Center batting on adhesive side of board; press into place. Center stitched piece on board and press edges onto adhesive. Trim edges close to board. Glue board inside screw ring.

Designs by Dick Martin.

Bee My Little Baby

48

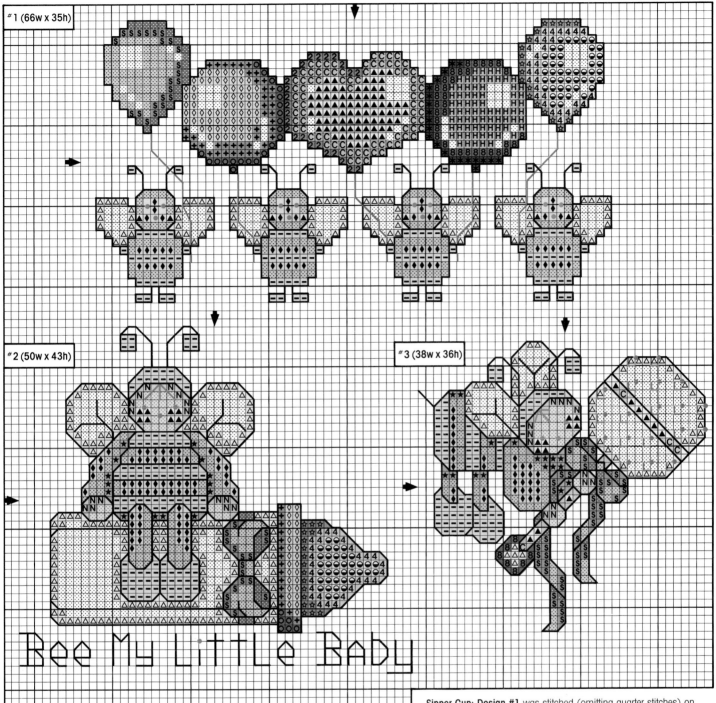

#1 (66w x 35h)

#2 (50w x 43h)

#3 (38w x 36h)

Bee My Little Baby

X	DMC	1/4 X	B'ST	ANC.	COLOR	X	DMC	1/4 X	B'ST	ANC.	COLOR
	blanc			2	white		725			305	yellow
O	209			109	dk purple	♦	727			293	lt yellow
+	210			108	purple		754			1012	lt flesh
◊	211			342	lt purple	N	758			882	flesh
−	310	◢	╱	403	black	△	775			128	vy lt blue
✱	322		╱	978	dk blue	★	783			307	dk yellow
8	334	◢		977	blue		801		╱	359	brown
☆	351	◢		10	dk peach	2	961			76	dk pink
4	352	◢		9	peach	C	962			75	pink
◗	353			6	lt peach	H	3325			129	lt blue
▨	562	◢		210	dk green	▲	3716			25	lt pink
S	563	◢	╱	208	green	●	209				dk purple French Knot
	564	◢		206	lt green	●	310				black French Knot

Sipper Cup: Design #1 was stitched (omitting quarter stitches) on a 7 1/2" x 3" piece of Vinyl-Weave™ (14 ct). Three strands of floss were used for Cross Stitch and 1 for Backstitch and French Knots. It was inserted in a Stitch-A-Sipper™. Hand wash sipper to protect stitchery.

Bottle Warmer: A portion of Design #1 (refer to photo) was stitched on the White Aida (14 ct) border of a purchased bottle warmer. Three strands of floss were used for Cross Stitch and 1 for Backstitch and French Knots.

Pillow: Design #2 was stitched on a White Aida (14 ct) prefinished pillow. Three strands of floss were used for Backstitch and French Knots.

Romper: Design #2 was stitched (omitting words) over a 5" x 6" piece of 14 mesh waste canvas on a purchased romper. Three strands of floss were used for Cross Stitch and 1 for Backstitch and French Knots. See Working on Waste Canvas, page 143.

Bib: Design #3 was stitched on a White Aida (14 ct) purchased baby bib. Three strands of floss were used for Cross Stitch and 1 for Backstitch and French Knots.

Designs by Lorri Birmingham.

FUN BOOKMARKS

Boys and girls will enjoy using our fun bookmarks! Stitched on sturdy Vinyl-Weave™, each page keeper features an encouraging message and a cute coordinating motif. The simple designs are quick and easy to finish, too.

Reading always carries me away

It's a purr-fect day for reading a book!

Books are buzzing with new ideas!

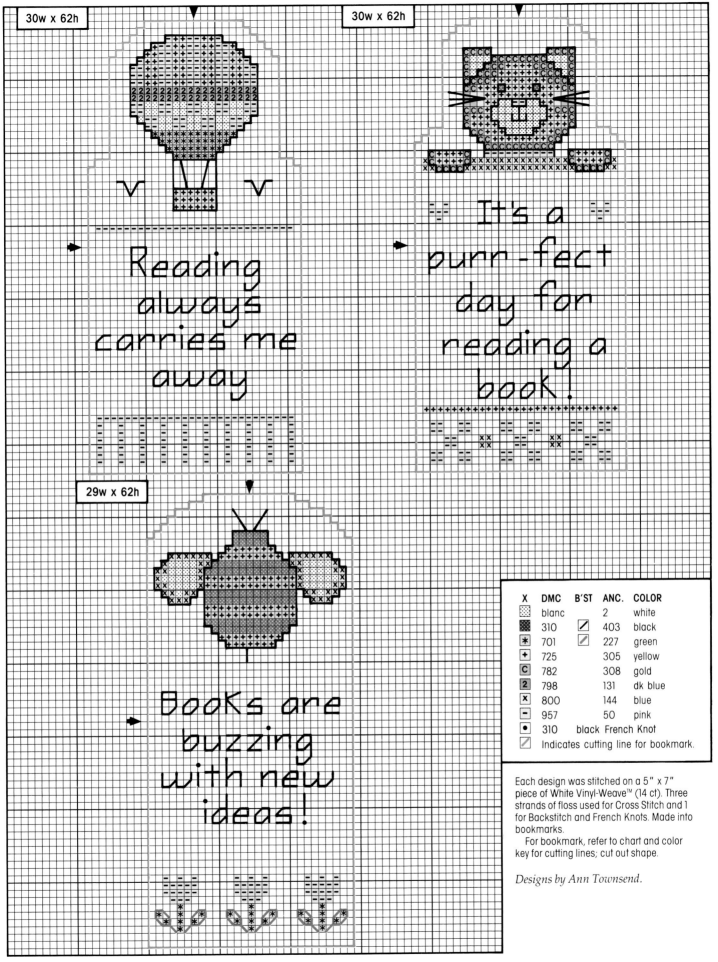

30w x 62h

30w x 62h

Reading always carries me away

It's a purr-fect day for reading a book!

29w x 62h

Books are buzzing with new ideas!

X	DMC	B'ST	ANC.	COLOR
	blanc		2	white
	310	✓	403	black
*	701	✓	227	green
+	725		305	yellow
C	782		308	gold
2	798		131	dk blue
x	800		144	blue
-	957		50	pink
●	310		black	French Knot
✓	Indicates cutting line for bookmark.			

Each design was stitched on a 5" x 7" piece of White Vinyl-Weave™ (14 ct). Three strands of floss used for Cross Stitch and 1 for Backstitch and French Knots. Made into bookmarks.

For bookmark, refer to chart and color key for cutting lines; cut out shape.

Designs by Ann Townsend.

PRECIOUS BABY GIFTS

*Celebrating the arrival of a new baby, our lovable
little animals embellish an afghan and a onesie
for naptime and a bib and sipper cup for mealtime.
These precious keepsakes will make sweet gift sets.*

52

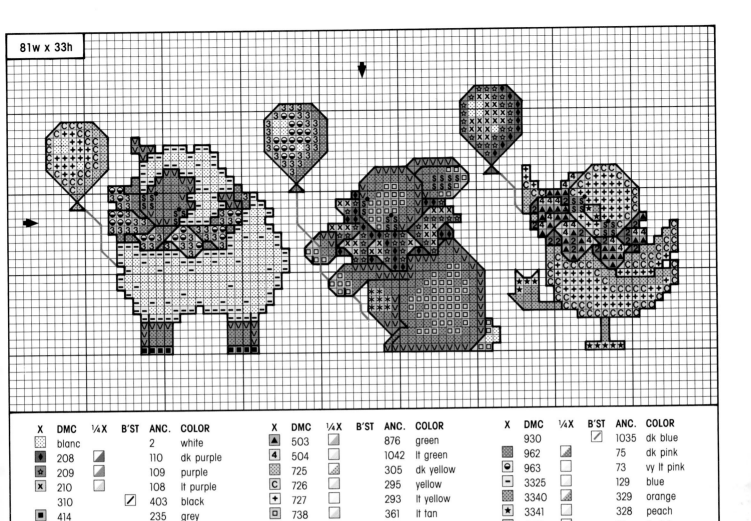

81w x 33h

X	DMC	1/4X	B'ST	ANC.	COLOR	X	DMC	1/4X	B'ST	ANC.	COLOR	X	DMC	1/4X	B'ST	ANC.	COLOR
	blanc			2	white	▲	503			876	green		930		/	1035	dk blue
◆	208	/		110	dk purple	4	504			1042	lt green		962	/		75	dk pink
★	209	/		109	purple		725	/		305	dk yellow	◔	963			73	vy lt pink
x	210	/		108	lt purple	C	726			295	yellow	-	3325			129	blue
	310		/	403	black	+	727			293	lt yellow		3340	/		329	orange
■	414			235	grey	□	738			361	lt tan	★	3341			328	peach
V	436	/		1045	dk tan	*	739			387	beige	3	3716	/		25	lt pink
	437	/		362	tan	S	760			1022	pink	•	310				black French Knot
2	502	/		877	dk green												

Afghan: Design was stitched twice over 2 fabric threads on a 29" x 45" piece (baby afghan size) of Soft White Anne Cloth (18 ct). Six strands of floss used for Cross Stitch and 2 for Backstitch and French Knots.

For fringe, cut off selvage of fabric. Machine stitch along woven stripe around outside edge of afghan. Fringe fabric to machine-stitched lines. Refer to Diagram to place design on fabric.

Bib: Bunny **only** was stitched on a prefinished baby bib. Three strands of floss used for Cross Stitch and 1 for Backstitch and French Knots.

Romper: Lamb **only** was stitched over a 6" x 7" piece of 10 mesh waste canvas on a white romper. Three strands of floss used for Cross Stitch and 1 for Backstitch and French Knots.

Sipper Cup: Baby Chick **only** was centered and stitched (omitting quarter stitches) on a 7½" x 3" piece of Vinyl-Weave™ (14 ct). Three strands of floss used for Cross Stitch and 1 for Backstitch and French Knots. Inserted in a Stitch-A-Sipper™. Hand wash to protect stitchery.

Design by Lorri Birmingham.

Working On Waste Canvas: Waste canvas is a special canvas that provides an evenweave grid for placing stitches on fabric. After the design is worked over the canvas, the canvas threads are removed, leaving the design on the fabric. The canvas is available in several mesh sizes.

1. Cover edges of canvas with masking tape. Cut a piece of lightweight, non-fusible interfacing the same size as the canvas to provide a firm stitching base.
2. Find desired stitching area on garment and mark center of area with a pin. Match center of canvas to pin on garment. With canvas threads straight, pin canvas to garment; pin interfacing to wrong side. Baste all three thicknesses together (**Fig. 1**).
3. Using a sharp needle, work design, stitching from large holes to large holes.
4. Trim canvas to within ¾" of design. Dampen canvas until it becomes limp. Pull out canvas threads one at a time using tweezers (**Fig. 2**). Trim interfacing close to design.

Fig. 1

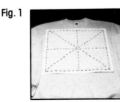

Fig. 2

DIAGRAM

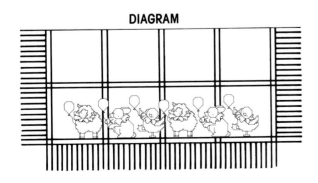

*Little lambs and colorful balloons accent this sweet
collection for baby. The set will make a charming
gift for a new mother and her "cutie pie."*

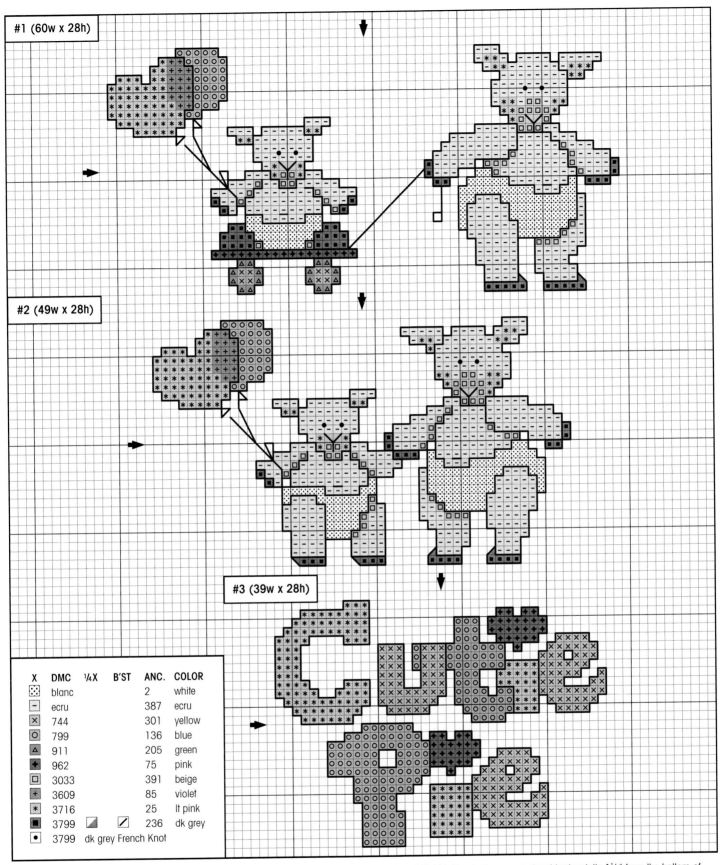

X	DMC	¼X	B'ST	ANC.	COLOR
blanc				2	white
-	ecru			387	ecru
X	744			301	yellow
O	799			136	blue
△	911			205	green
+	962			75	pink
□	3033			391	beige
+	3609			85	violet
*	3716			25	lt pink
■	3799	◣	╱	236	dk grey
•	3799		dk grey French Knot		

#1 (60w x 28h)

#2 (49w x 28h)

#3 (39w x 28h)

Note: All projects were stitched using 3 strands of floss for Cross Stitch and 1 for Backstitch and French Knots.
Bib: Designs #2 and #3 were each centered and stitched on the Blue Aida (14 ct) insert of a purchased bib.
Towel: Design #1 was stitched on the 14 ct border of a Light Blue Velour Fingertip™ towel.
T-Shirt: Design #2 was stitched over a 5" square of 14 mesh waste canvas on a purchased T-shirt. The design was centered horizontally 1½" from the bottom of neckband. See Working on Waste Canvas, page 143.
Diaper Cover: Design #3 was stitched over a 5" square of 14 mesh waste canvas on a purchased diaper cover. The design was centered horizontally 4" from the bottom of waistband. See Working on Waste Canvas, page 143.

Designs by Terrie Lee Steinmeyer,©1996

These super stick-ups are perfect for displaying your favorite youngsters' artwork or photos. The sunny collection includes a variety of messages to let kids know you think they're great! There's a magnet for your grocery list, too.

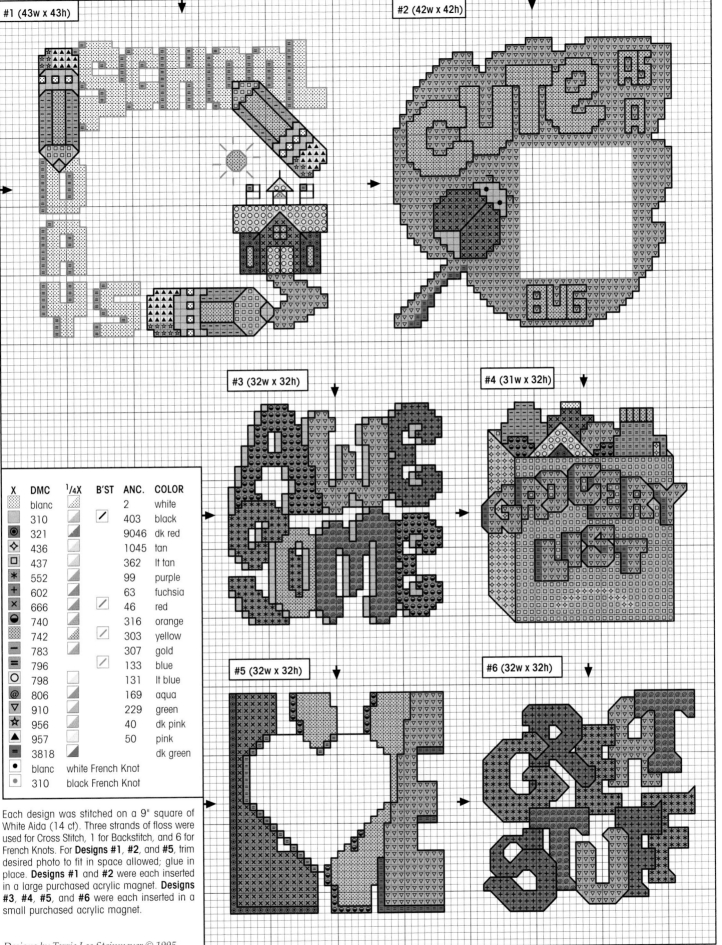

#1 (43w x 43h)   #2 (42w x 42h)

#3 (32w x 32h)   #4 (31w x 32h)

#5 (32w x 32h)   #6 (32w x 32h)

X	DMC	1/4X	B'ST	ANC.	COLOR
	blanc			2	white
	310		/	403	black
◉	321			9046	dk red
◈	436			1045	tan
▢	437			362	lt tan
✳	552			99	purple
➕	602			63	fuchsia
✕	666		/	46	red
◖	740			316	orange
▦	742		/	303	yellow
▬	783			307	gold
＝	796		/	133	blue
◯	798			131	lt blue
@	806			169	aqua
▽	910			229	green
★	956			40	dk pink
▲	957			50	pink
▤	3818				dk green
●	blanc				white French Knot
●	310				black French Knot

Each design was stitched on a 9" square of White Aida (14 ct). Three strands of floss were used for Cross Stitch, 1 for Backstitch, and 6 for French Knots. For **Designs #1, #2,** and **#5,** trim desired photo to fit in space allowed; glue in place. **Designs #1** and **#2** were each inserted in a large purchased acrylic magnet. **Designs #3, #4, #5,** and **#6** were each inserted in a small purchased acrylic magnet.

Designs by Terrie Lee Steinmeyer © 1995.

MEALTIME FUN

Make breakfast, lunch, and dinner fun for baby with these three cute sets of bibs and cups.

I'm Egg-cited
About Breakfast

I can bearly
wait for
Dinner

I have a hunch
about lunch

X	DMC	¼X	B'ST	X	DMC	¼X	B'ST	X	DMC	B'ST
•	blanc			❖	743			■	3371	
★	309			=	744			◉	3755	
	322			○	775			•	322	French Knot
+	335			◆	912			•	912	French Knot
✳	436			$	954			⊘	912	Lazy Daisy
▽	437			★	3340					
▢	739			✔	3341					

With quips advertising "Ark Repair," "Rainbow Construction," and "Free Estimates," Noah's happy crew delivers a rainbow of fun on this plump pillow. The colorful cushion makes an ideal accent for the nursery!

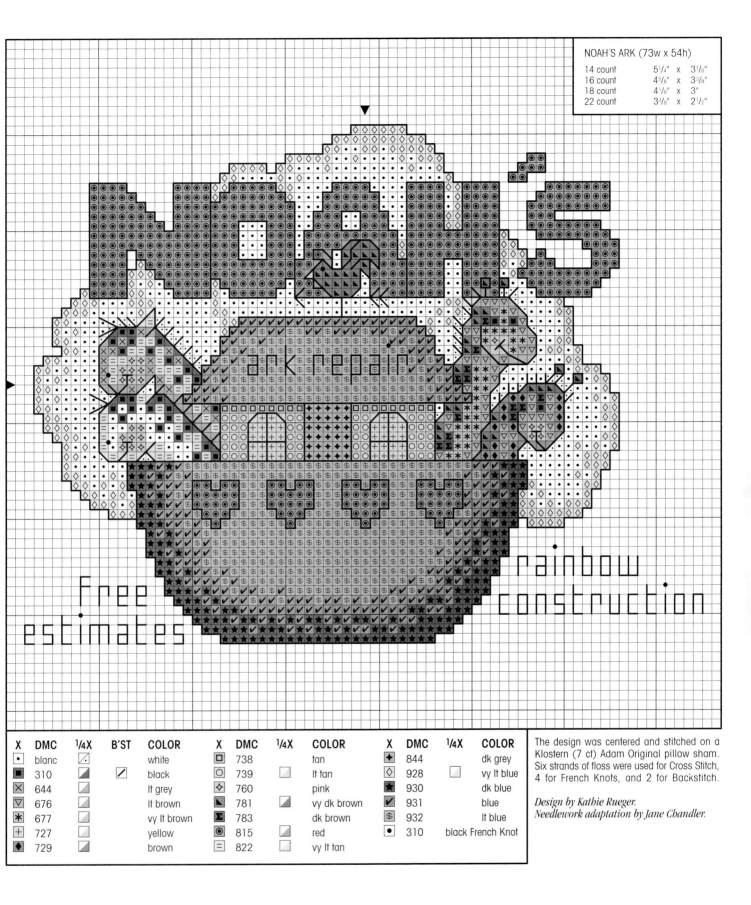

NOAH'S ARK (73w x 54h)		
14 count	5¼"	x	3⅞"
16 count	4⅝"	x	3⅜"
18 count	4⅛"	x	3"
22 count	3⅜"	x	2½"

X	DMC	¼X	B'ST	COLOR	X	DMC	¼X	COLOR	X	DMC	¼X	COLOR
•	blanc			white	□	738		tan	✛	844		dk grey
■	310		/	black	○	739		lt tan	◇	928		vy lt blue
✕	644			lt grey	✦	760		pink	★	930		dk blue
▽	676			lt brown	◣	781		vy dk brown	✔	931		blue
✳	677			vy lt brown	Σ	783		dk brown	$	932		lt blue
✛	727			yellow	◉	815		red	●	310		black French Knot
◆	729			brown	=	822		vy lt tan				

The design was centered and stitched on a Klostern (7 ct) Adam Original pillow sham. Six strands of floss were used for Cross Stitch, 4 for French Knots, and 2 for Backstitch.

Design by Kathie Rueger.
Needlework adaptation by Jane Chandler.

61

*These adorable cover-ups remind us of what little girls and
boys are made of. A thoughtful and useful gift, each set includes
a bib for baby and a burping towel for Mom's shoulder.*

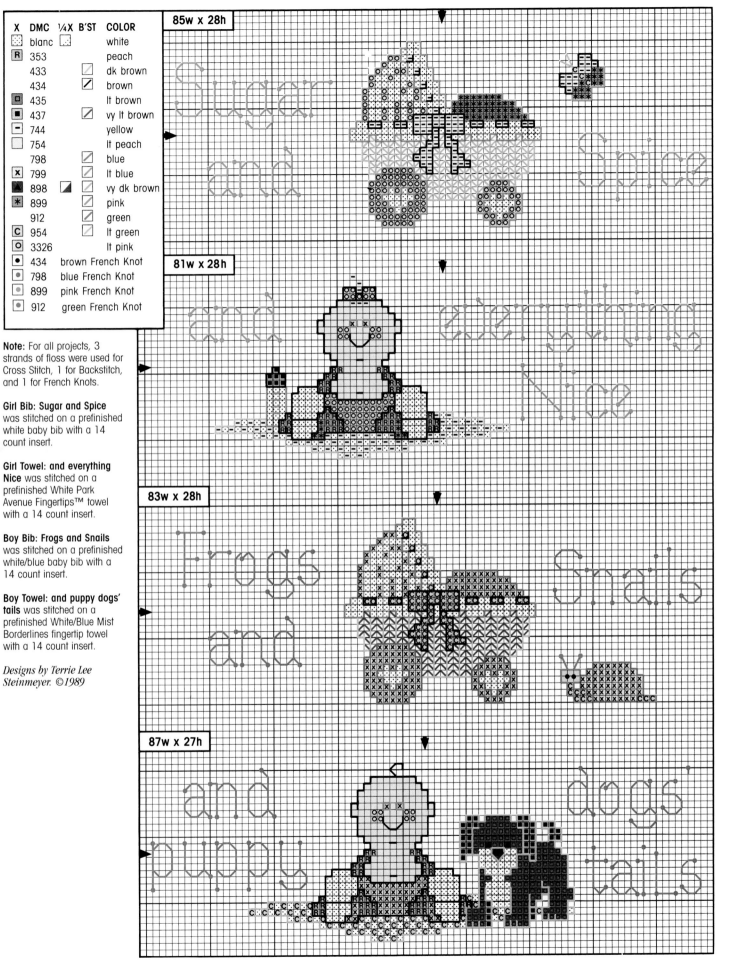

X	DMC	¼X	B'ST	COLOR
	blanc			white
R	353			peach
	433		✓	dk brown
	434		✓	brown
	435			lt brown
	437		✓	vy lt brown
-	744			yellow
	754			lt peach
	798		✓	blue
X	799		✓	lt blue
	898	✓	✓	vy dk brown
*	899		✓	pink
	912		✓	green
C	954		✓	lt green
O	3326			lt pink
•	434			brown French Knot
•	798			blue French Knot
•	899			pink French Knot
•	912			green French Knot

Note: For all projects, 3 strands of floss were used for Cross Stitch, 1 for Backstitch, and 1 for French Knots.

Girl Bib: Sugar and Spice was stitched on a prefinished white baby bib with a 14 count insert.

Girl Towel: and everything Nice was stitched on a prefinished White Park Avenue Fingertips™ towel with a 14 count insert.

Boy Bib: Frogs and Snails was stitched on a prefinished white/blue baby bib with a 14 count insert.

Boy Towel: and puppy dogs' tails was stitched on a prefinished White/Blue Mist Borderlines fingertip towel with a 14 count insert.

Designs by Terrie Lee Steinmeyer. ©1989

85w x 28h

81w x 28h

83w x 28h

87w x 27h

Swift Gifts
FOR ALL

It's easy to find the perfect gift for your loved ones with this super collection! You can create tailor-made presents for everyone you know — for every taste or interest. You'll find sporty caps for Dad, a wedding sampler for newlyweds, and some great gifts for teacher, along with mugs, magnets, and more. Stitched on prefinished bookmarks, these Happy Birthday Flowers can be used to send birthday greetings all through the year. Your friends and family will think you have gift-giving down to an art!

65

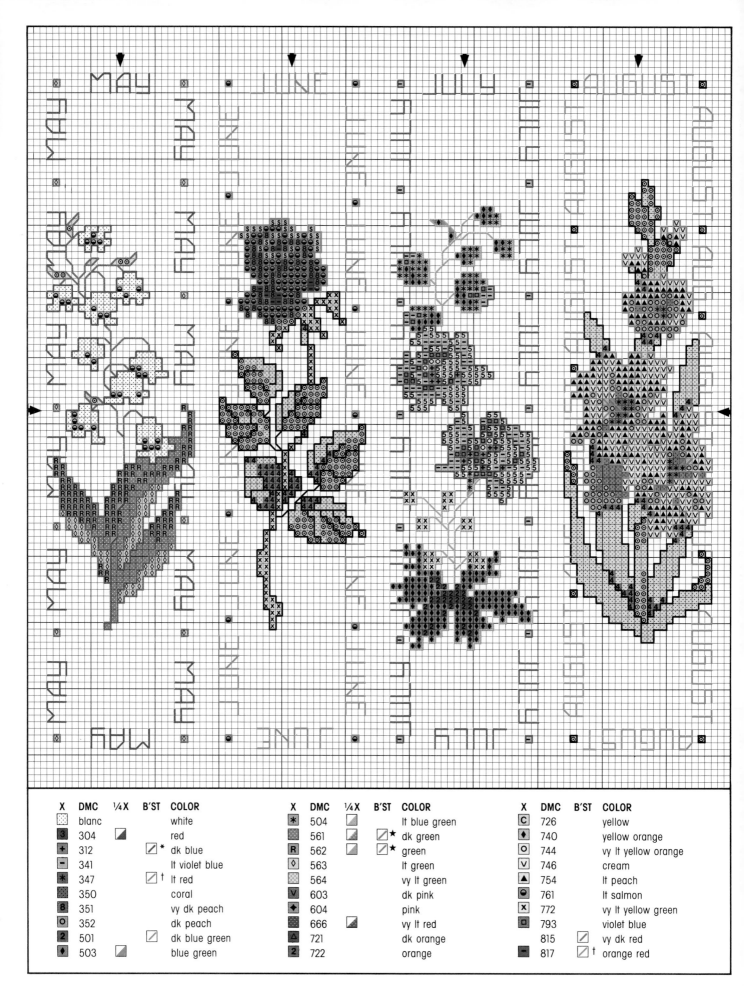

X	DMC	¼X	B'ST	COLOR	X	DMC	¼X	B'ST	COLOR	X	DMC	B'ST	COLOR
░	blanc			white	✳	504	◩		lt blue green	C	726		yellow
3	304	◩		red	▨	561	◩		dk green	◆	740		yellow orange
+	312		◩ *	dk blue	R	562	◩	◩★	green	O	744		vy lt yellow orange
−	341			lt violet blue	◇	563			lt green	V	746		cream
✳	347		◩ †	lt red	▨	564			vy lt green	▲	754		lt peach
▨	350			coral	V	603			dk pink	◓	761		lt salmon
8	351			vy dk peach	◆	604			pink	x	772		vy lt yellow green
O	352			dk peach	▨	666		◪	vy lt red	▥	793		violet blue
2	501		◩	dk blue green	▲	721			dk orange		815	◩	vy dk red
◆	503	◩		blue green	2	722			orange		817	◩ †	orange red

66

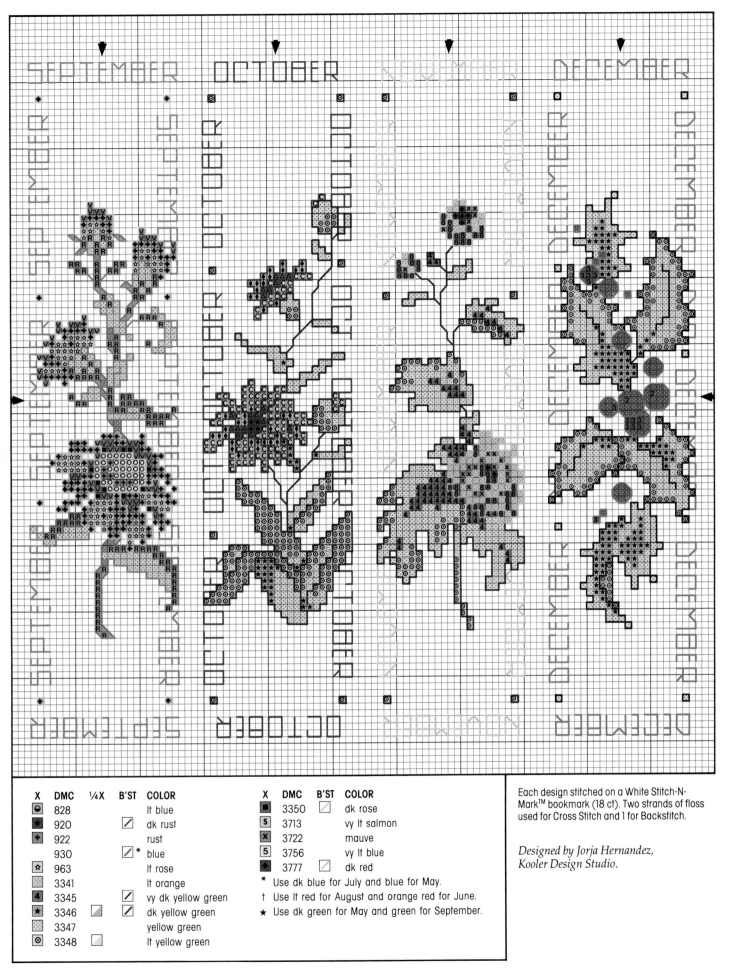

X	DMC	¼X	B'ST	COLOR
◒	828			lt blue
★	920		✓	dk rust
✛	922			rust
	930		✓ *	blue
☆	963			lt rose
	3341			lt orange
4	3345		✓	vy dk yellow green
★	3346	◫	✓	dk yellow green
	3347			yellow green
⊙	3348	◻		lt yellow green

X	DMC	B'ST	COLOR
■	3350	✓	dk rose
S	3713		vy lt salmon
X	3722		mauve
5	3756		vy lt blue
◆	3777	✓	dk red

* Use dk blue for July and blue for May.

† Use lt red for August and orange red for June.

★ Use dk green for May and green for September.

Each design stitched on a White Stitch-N-Mark™ bookmark (18 ct). Two strands of floss used for Cross Stitch and 1 for Backstitch.

Designed by Jorja Hernandez, Kooler Design Studio.

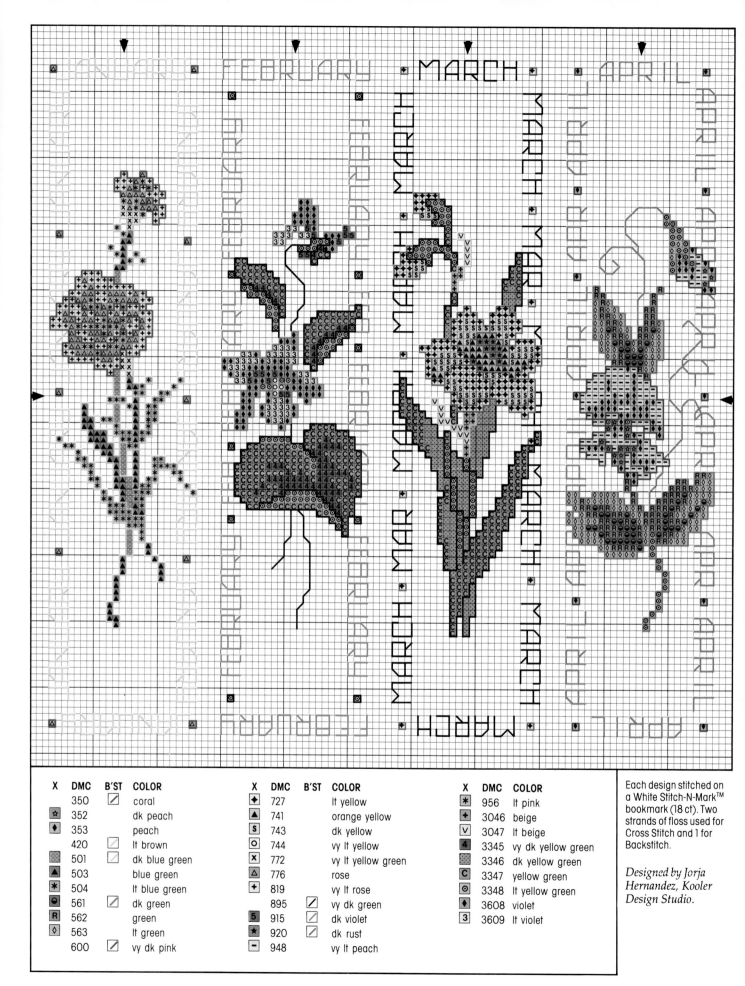

X	DMC	B'ST	COLOR
	350	∕	coral
★	352		dk peach
◆	353		peach
	420	∕	lt brown
▦	501	∕	dk blue green
▲	503		blue green
✳	504		lt blue green
◕	561	∕	dk green
R	562		green
◇	563		lt green
	600	∕	vy dk pink

X	DMC	B'ST	COLOR
✦	727		lt yellow
▲	741		orange yellow
S	743		dk yellow
◎	744		vy lt yellow
X	772		vy lt yellow green
△	776		rose
✛	819		vy lt rose
	895	∕	vy dk green
5	915		dk violet
★	920		dk rust
–	948		vy lt peach

X	DMC	COLOR
✳	956	lt pink
✛	3046	beige
V	3047	lt beige
4	3345	vy dk yellow green
▒	3346	dk yellow green
C	3347	yellow green
◉	3348	lt yellow green
◆	3608	violet
3	3609	lt violet

Each design stitched on a White Stitch-N-Mark™ bookmark (18 ct). Two strands of floss used for Cross Stitch and 1 for Backstitch.

Designed by Jorja Hernandez, Kooler Design Studio.

ZODIAC MUGS

When you need a quick gift, look to the stars for inspiration! Featuring the twelve signs of the zodiac, these mugs make perfect presents for all your friends and family.

ZODIAC MUGS (40w x 40h)

X	DMC	B'ST	JPC	COLOR		X	DMC		JPC	COLOR		X	DMC		JPC	COLOR		X	DMC		JPC	COLOR		X	DMC	B'ST	JPC	COLOR
★	310	⟋	8403	black			351		3011	peach		2	725		2298	yellow		◇	909	⟋*	6228	dk green
♦	321	⟋*	3500	red		S	353		3006	lt peach		4	742		2303	dk yellow		⊖	911		6205	green
3	333	⟋		purple		▣	553		4097	lt purple		N	745		2296	lt yellow		★	946		2330	orange
	347	⟋†	3013	dk salmon		X	564		6209	lt green		✱	783		5307	gold		◉	970		2327	lt orange
▬	349		2335	orange red		✦	718			pink purple		△	798		7022	blue			975	⟋*	5349	brown

X	DMC	B'ST	JPC	COLOR
▲	3705	☑ †	3012	salmon
∨	3712			lt salmon
◆	3755			lt blue
◎	3765	☑ ★		dk green blue

* Use red for Aries, dk green for Taurus and Capricorn, and brown for Leo.

† Use dk salmon for Virgo and salmon for Pisces.

★ Use lt purple for Cancer and dk green blue for Libra.

Each design stitched on a 10½" x 3½" piece of Vinyl-Weave® (14 ct). Three strands of floss used for Cross Stitch and 1 for Backstitch. Inserted in a Stitch-A-Mug™.

Place design on Vinyl-Weave® 1¼" from desired short edge and ³⁄₈" from bottom edge. Place Vinyl-Weave® in mug with short edges of vinyl aligned with handle.

Hand wash mug to protect stitchery.

Designs by Holly DeFount.

You can give your loved ones a watchful pair of guardian angels when you present each of them with this precious key ring. Because the design is so quick and easy to stitch, you'll have time to create a host of these heavenly helpers for family and friends — and yourself, too!

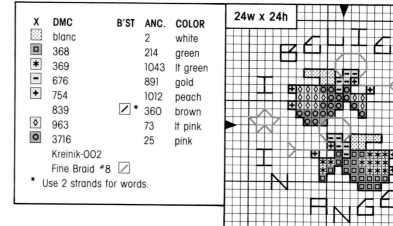

The design was stitched on a 2¼" diameter piece of Vinyl-Weave™ (14 ct). Three strands of floss were used for Cross Stitch and 1 for Backstitch (unless otherwise noted in the color key). It was inserted in a purchased key ring.

Design by Deborah Lambein.

X	DMC	B'ST	ANC.	COLOR
▦	blanc		2	white
▣	368		214	green
✳	369		1043	lt green
−	676		891	gold
✚	754		1012	peach
	839	╱*	360	brown
◇	963		73	lt pink
◉	3716		25	pink
	Kreinik-002			
	Fine Braid #8	╱		

* Use 2 strands for words.

24w x 24h

HEARTFELT TRIBUTES

From A to Z, our mini pillows of affection let you fill in the blanks with the names of your loved ones. These quick-to-finish gifts can be attached to packages, jars, or baskets, or stuffed with potpourri for sweet-smelling sachets.

HEARTFELT TRIBUTES (41w x 24h)		
14 count	3"	x 1¾"
16 count	2⅝"	x 1½"
18 count	2⅜"	x 1⅜"
22 count	1⅞"	x 1⅛"

X	DMC	ANC.	COLOR
★	3731	76	pink
△	3733	75	lt pink
◇	3768	779	blue

Design stitched on a 7" x 6" piece of Antique White Aida (14 ct). Three strands of floss used for Cross Stitch. To personalize, use alphabet provided. Made into a mini pillow.

For each mini pillow, trim stitched piece 1" larger than design on all sides. Cut a piece of Antique White Aida the same size as stitched piece for backing. With wrong sides facing, use 2 strands of blue floss and Running Stitches to join fabric pieces together ½" from bottom and side edges. Stuff with polyester fiberfill. Repeat to stitch across top of mini pillow ½" from edge. Fringe fabric to within one square of stitched lines.

Designed by Margaret Manderfeld.

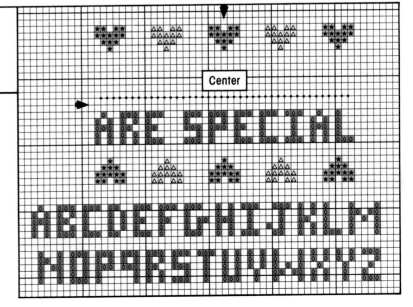

73

Want to make a top-rate Father's Day gift? Stitch him one of these sporty caps! We've given you three designs with sports themes, plus one to let Dad know you think he's the best.

#1.
57w x 30h

#2.
63w x 35h

#3.
64w x 34h

#4.
65w x 33h

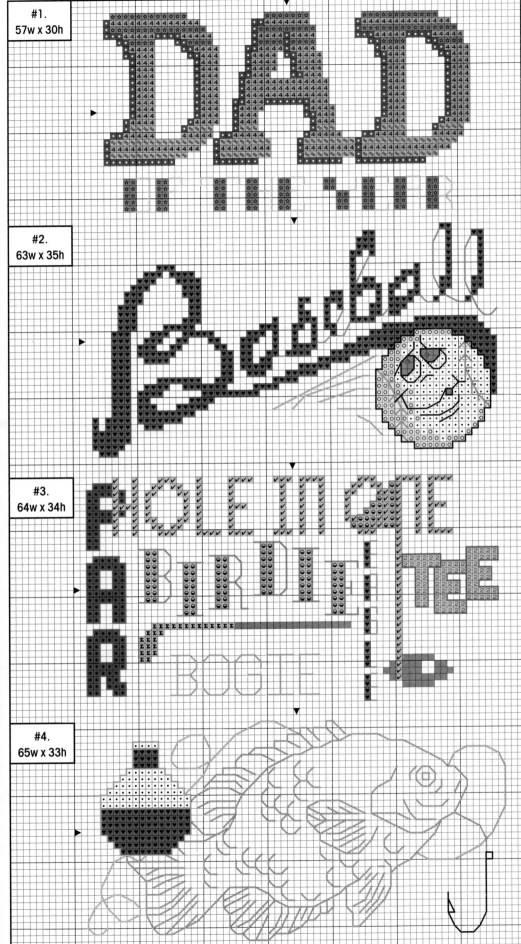

X	DMC	¼X	B'ST	COLOR
•	blanc	·		white
☆	312		/	lt navy
4	322			vy dk blue
✳	334		/	dk blue
•	336			navy
Σ	414			grey
✓	700			green
○	775			vy lt blue
	783		/	gold
♥	817		/	red
	839		/	brown
	931		/	grey blue
⊖	973			yellow
2	3325			lt blue
%	3755			blue
	3799	◨	/	dk grey
•	blanc			white French Knot

Hat Designs #1, #2, and **#4** were stitched on sportsman hats with White Aida (14 ct) inserts and **Design #3** was stitched on a golf hat with White Aida (14 ct) insert by Crafter's Pride. Two strands of floss were used for Cross Stitch and 1 for all other stitches.

Designs by Sam Hawkins.

75

Presented to a special couple on their wedding day, this simple marriage sampler will remind them to always keep their hearts filled with love. The motif from the sampler can also be used to create a coordinating rice bag.

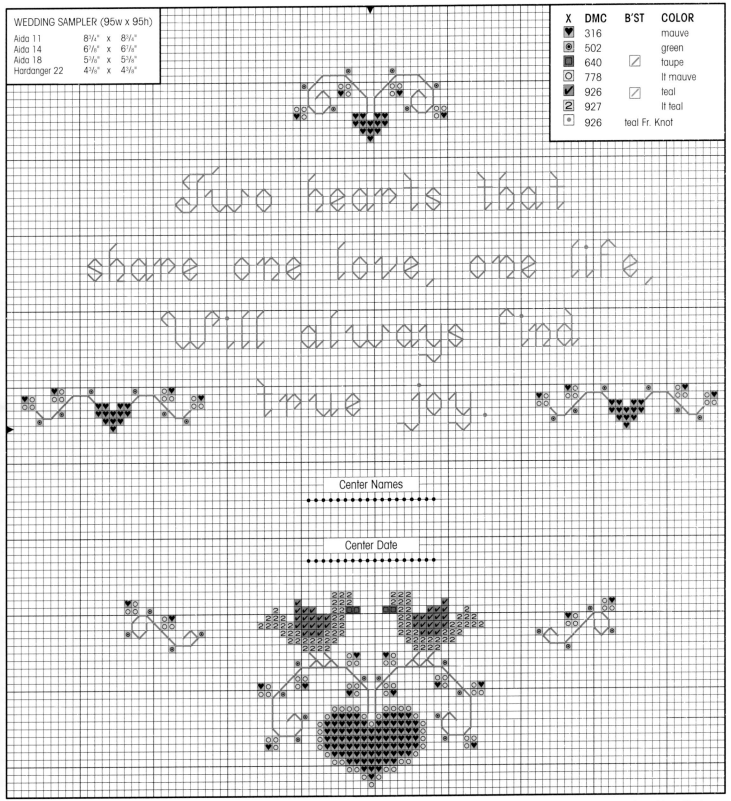

X	DMC	B'ST	COLOR
♥	316		mauve
⊙	502		green
◨	640	╱	taupe
O	778		lt mauve
✔	926	╱	teal
2	927		lt teal
•	926		teal Fr. Knot

WEDDING SAMPLER (95w x 95h)

Aida 11	8³/₄"	x	8³/₄"
Aida 14	6⁷/₈"	x	6⁷/₈"
Aida 18	5³/₈"	x	5³/₈"
Hardanger 22	4³/₈"	x	4³/₈"

Center Names

Center Date

Hoop: We stitched the **Wedding Sampler** on a 10" x 10" piece of Ivory Aida (14 ct). We used 2 strands of floss for Cross Stitch, 1 for Backstitch and 1 for French Knots. To personalize, stitch names and date using DMC 640 floss and alphabets and numbers provided on page 144. It was inserted in an 8" dia. wooden hoop. For Hoop, cut Batting and backing fabric same size as stitched piece. Place batting between backing fabric and stitched piece. Insert in hoop, pulling materials taut. Trim materials close to hoop. Glue 1¹/₂" w ecru pre-gathered eyelet to back of hoop. For ruffle, cut a 5"w x 59"l piece of fabric. Turn short ends ¹/₂" to wrong side; press. Fold strip in half lengthwise with wrong sides together; press. Baste close to raw edge. Make another basting seam ¹/₄" from the first; pull basting threads. Glue ruffle to eyelet. Trim as desired.

Rice Bag: We stitched the lower section of design on a 4" x 5" piece of Ivory Hardanger (22 ct). It was centered with bottom of design 1" from one short edge of fabric. We used 1 strand of floss for Cross Stitch and 1 for Backstitch. For backing, cut a second 4" x 5" piece of Hardanger. Fold an 18" length of ¹/₁₆" w ribbon in half. On right side of stitched piece, 1¹/₂" from top, pin folded edge of ribbon to left raw edge. With right sides together and beginning and ending seam ¹/₂" from top edge, sew fabrics together along sides and bottom using a ¹/₂" seam allowance. Turn right side out and fringe top edge ¹/₂".

Design by Mary Scott.

77

These A⁺ gifts will make teacher feel appreciated! The cute surprises include a mug, a bookmark, a lid for topping a jar of chalk, a sampler, and a blackboard eraser cover.

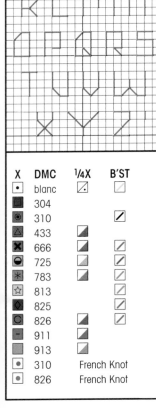

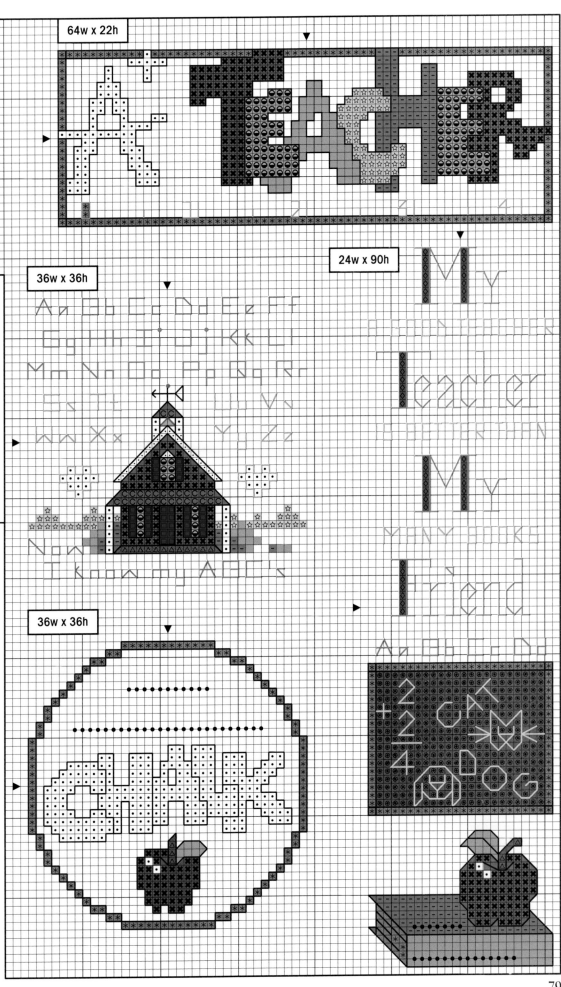

64w x 22h

24w x 90h

36w x 36h

36w x 36h

X	DMC	¼X	B'ST
•	blanc	◿	◿
◼	304		
◉	310		◿
◮	433	◿	◿
✕	666	◿	◿
◒	725	◿	◿
✳	783	◿	◿
☆	813		◿
◈	825		◿
◯	826	◿	◿
–	911	◿	
▨	913	◿	
⦿	310		French Knot
⦿	826		French Knot

A+ Teacher: Stitched on a 9" x 6" piece of Black Aida (14 ct). Four strands of floss used for Cross Stitch and 1 for Backstitch. Mounted on cardboard; glued to a blackboard eraser. **Also stitched** on a 10½" x 3½" piece of Vinyl-Weave® (14 ct). Three strands of floss used for Cross Stitch and 1 for Backstitch. Inserted in a Stitch-A-Mug™.

Chalk: Stitched on a 7" square of Black Aida (14 ct). Four strands of floss used for Cross Stitch, 2 for 666 Backstitch, and 1 for 310 Backstitch. Inserted in wide-mouth jar lid. Center and stitch name on dotted lines with 666 Backstitch using Alphabet.

My Teacher, My Friend: Stitched on a White Stitch-N-Mark™ Bookmark (18 ct). Two strands of floss used for Cross Stitch and 1 for Backstitch. Stitch name on dotted lines on book with 310 Backstitch using alphabet from Schoolhouse Sampler.

Schoolhouse Sampler: Stitched on a 9" square of White Aida (14 ct). Three strands of floss used for Cross Stitch and 1 for all other stitches. Custom framed.

Designs by *Terrie Lee Steinmeyer*

FLORAL MINI CLOTHS

Here's a quick and inexpensive recipe for creating four charming gifts! Take one standard bread cloth: divide into fourths. Stitch one of these six dainty floral designs on each one; fringe the edges. Place cloths in miniature baskets and fill with goodies. Serves four special friends.

Floral Mini Cloth designs were stitched on corners of mini bread cloths, 4 fabric threads from beginning of fringe. Two strands of floss were used for Cross Stitch and 1 for all other stitches. They were inserted in small market baskets approx. 2" deep x 3" wide x 4¹/₂" long (slightly smaller and larger baskets may also be used).

For four mini bread cloths, fold one Ivory Royal Classic (14 ct) Bread Cover in half with edges matched; cut along fold. Fold each half of bread cover in half with short edges matched; cut along fold. To complete fringe of each mini bread cloth, ravel 8 fabric threads from cut edges of mini bread cloth.

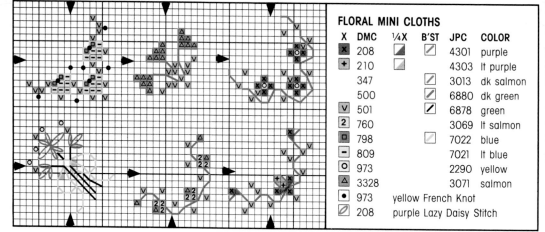

FLORAL MINI CLOTHS

X	DMC	¼X	B'ST	JPC	COLOR
☒	208	◤	◿	4301	purple
⊞	210	◤		4303	lt purple
	347		◿	3013	dk salmon
	500		◿	6880	dk green
☑	501		◿	6878	green
2	760			3069	lt salmon
☐	798		◿	7022	blue
−	809			7021	lt blue
⊙	973			2290	yellow
△	3328			3071	salmon
●	973				yellow French Knot
⊘	208				purple Lazy Daisy Stitch

80

QUILT-BLOCK BOOKMARKS

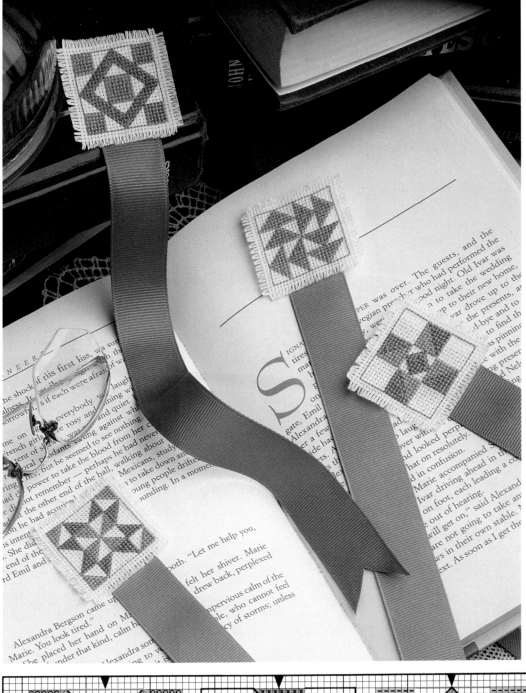

Your quilting friends will love these bookmarks featuring favorite quilt block patterns. The quick-to-finish markers make thoughtful little remembrances, whether they're used to reserve a spot in a novel or a needlework book!

Each design was stitched on a 5" square of Ivory Aida (18 ct). Two strands of floss were used for Cross Stitch and 1 for Backstitch.

For bookmark, trim stitched piece 4 squares from design edges. Fringe to 2 squares from design edges. Apply liquid fray preventative to base of fringe. Cut a 12" length of ⅞" w grosgrain ribbon; trim as desired and apply liquid fray preventative to ends. Glue one end of ribbon to center back of stitched piece.

Designed by Michele Crawford.

QUILT BLOCKS (24w x 24h)				
X	DMC	¼X	B'ST	COLOR
O	316			pink
–	502			green
x	931			blue

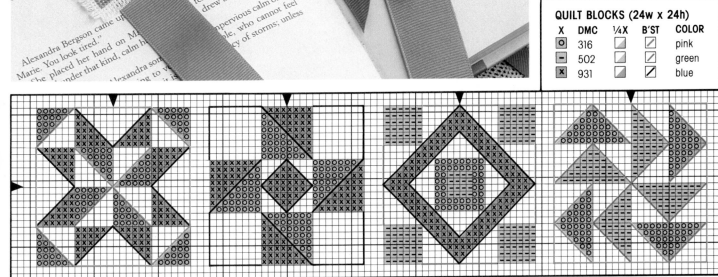

When just saying "thank you" isn't enough, why not give a jar of goodies topped with one of these cute designs? It's a sweet way to show your appreciation.

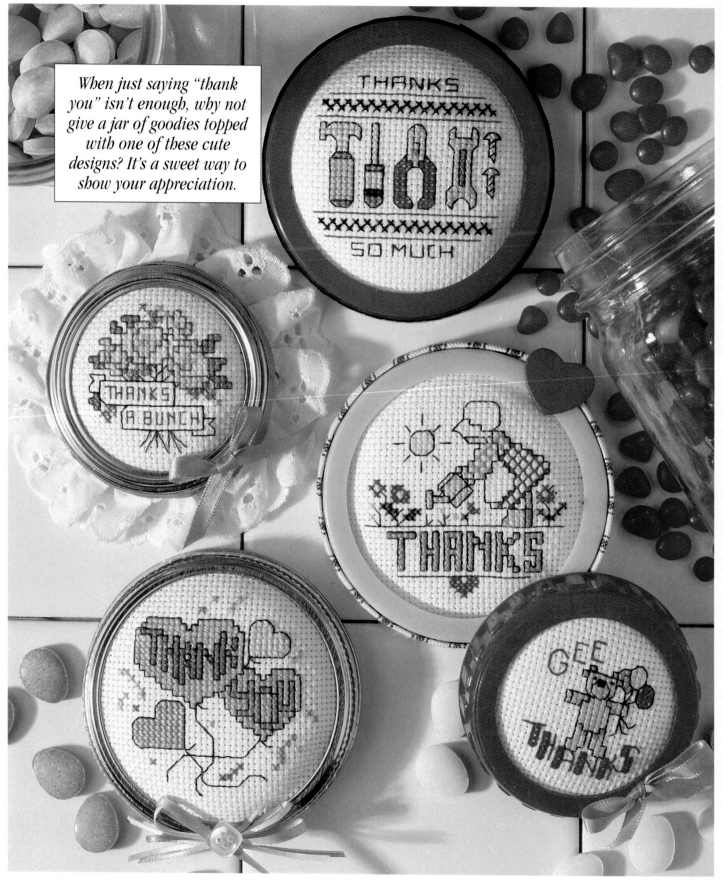

#1. (35w x 34h)

#2. (35w x 34h)

#3. (25w x 25h)

#4. (32w x 30h)

#5. (21w x 23h)

X	DMC	¼X	B'ST	JPC	COLOR
	blanc			1001	white
B	210			4303	purple
A	301				rust
C	319		✓	6246	dk green
X	320			6017	green
5	321		✓	3500	red
	326		✓	3401	dk rose
2	402				lt rust
V	414			8513	dk grey
R	415			8510	grey
*	436			5943	dk tan
★	603			3001	dk pink
□	604			3001	pink

X	DMC	¼X	B'ST	JPC	COLOR
3	727			2289	yellow
△	738			5375	tan
E	754			2331	peach
N	793				dk blue
★	794				blue
◆	899			3282	rose
◎	958			6186	dk aqua
▲	964			6185	lt aqua
−	3326			3126	lt pink
■	3371		✓	5478	brown black
4	3713				vy lt pink
•	3371			brown black French Knot	

Thank You jar lids were stitched on 6" squares of Antique White Aida (14 ct). Two strands of floss were used for Cross Stitch, 2 for red Backstitch in **Design #5**, 1 for all other Backstitch, and 1 for French Knots. **Designs #1, #2,** and **#4** were inserted into wide mouth jar lids; **Designs #3** and **#5** were inserted into small mouth jar lids.

For each jar lid, use outer edge of jar lid for pattern and cut a circle from adhesive mounting board. Using opening of jar lid for pattern, cut a circle of batting. Center batting on adhesive board and press in place. Center stitched piece on batting and press edges onto adhesive board; trim edges close to board. Glue board inside jar lid. Decorate as desired. (**Note:** Mason jar puff-up kits may be used to finish jar lids.)

Designed by Linda Gillum,
Kooler Design Studio.

Serve up some fun with our "I love ..." design for mugs! Just use the handy alphabet to cross stitch phrases that reflect the things your friends love the most. You'll never run out of ideas for creating one-of-a-kind gifts!

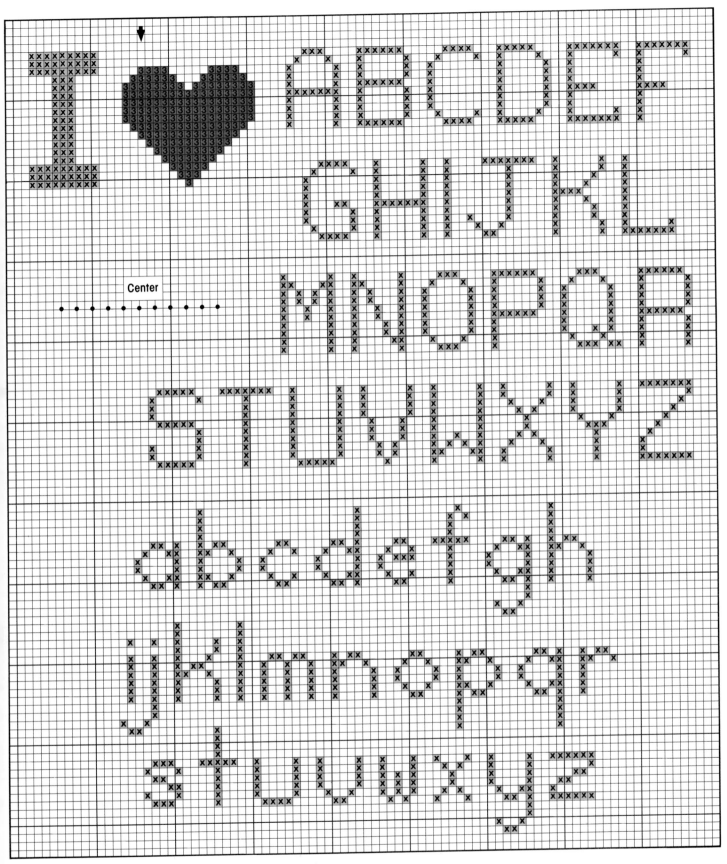

Mug designs were stitched on 3½" x 10¼" pieces of Vinyl-Weave® (14 ct). They were inserted in Stitch-A-Mugs from Charter Publishing.

Center design 3" from short edge of Vinyl-Weave® (right short edge for right handed person or left short edge for left handed person) and allowing approx. ⅝" from top edge. Three strands of floss were used for Cross Stitch.

Hand washing mug is recommended to protect the stitchery.

There's nothing that avid readers appreciate more than a good book — unless it's a bookmark to help them keep their place! The six delightful designs for prefinished corner markers in this collection will please everyone from grandmothers to grade-schoolers.

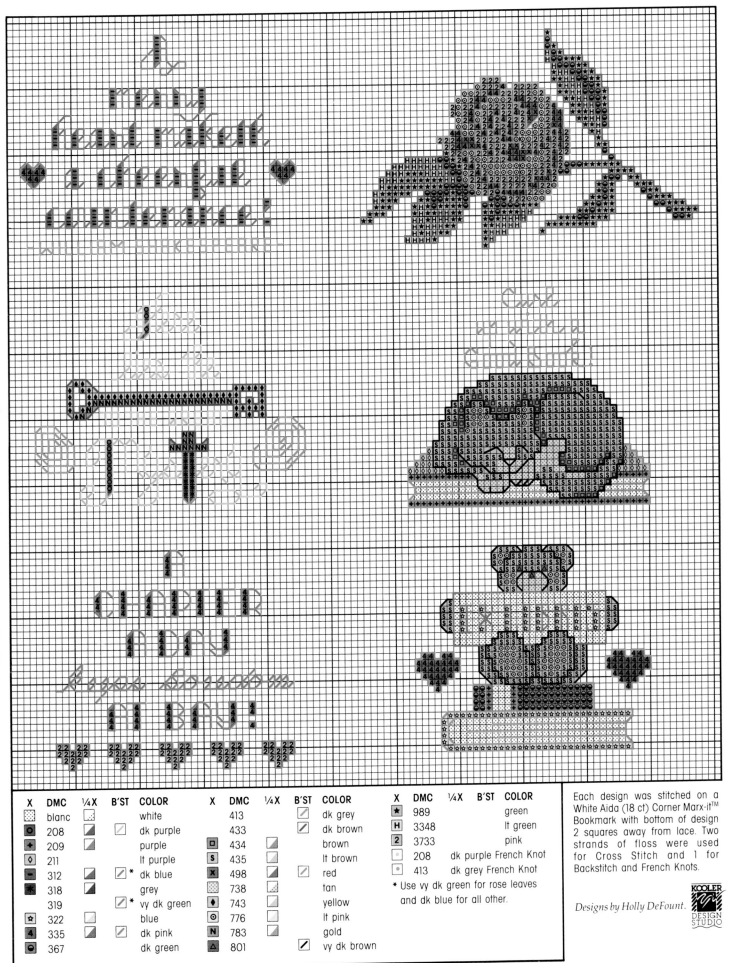

X	DMC	¼X	B'ST	COLOR	X	DMC	¼X	B'ST	COLOR	X	DMC	¼X	B'ST	COLOR
	blanc			white		413			dk grey	★	989			green
◉	208			dk purple		433			dk brown	H	3348			lt green
✦	209			purple	▫	434			brown	2	3733			pink
◇	211			lt purple	S	435			lt brown	·	208			dk purple French Knot
▬	312		✓*	dk blue	✗	498		✓	red	·	413			dk grey French Knot
✳	318			grey	▒	738			tan					
	319		✓*	vy dk green	◆	743			yellow	* Use vy dk green for rose leaves
☆	322			blue	⊙	776			lt pink	and dk blue for all other.
4	335		✓	dk pink	N	783			gold	
◒	367			dk green	△	801		✓	vy dk brown	

Each design was stitched on a White Aida (18 ct) Corner Marx-it™ Bookmark with bottom of design 2 squares away from lace. Two strands of floss were used for Cross Stitch and 1 for Backstitch and French Knots.

Designs by Holly DeFount.

BLUE RIBBON HONORS

Honor the special people in your life with jars of goodies topped with these blue-ribbon designs. Easy to stitch, the gifts will remind your family and friends that they're Number 1 with you.

The designs were stitched on 5" squares of Ivory Aida (14 ct). Refer to additional charts to stitch alternate names. Two strands of floss were used for Cross Stitch and 1 for Backstitch. They were inserted into wide mouth metal jar lids.

For each jar lid, use **outer edge** of jar lid for pattern and cut a circle from adhesive mounting board. Using **opening** of jar lid for pattern, cut a circle of batting. Center batting on adhesive board and press in place. Center stitched piece on batting and press edges onto adhesive board; trim edges close to board. Glue board inside jar lid. (**Note**: Mason jar puff-up kits may be used to finish jar lids.)
Designed by Donna Kooler Design Studios.

#1 JAR LIDS (33w x 33h)

X	DMC	B'ST	JPC	COLOR
O	680	✓	2876	gold
	745	✓*	2350	lt gold
C	825	✓	7181	dk blue
X	826		7180	blue
S	827		7159	lt blue

* Work in long stitches.

MOTORHOME MAGNETS

Free spirits who call the road their home will roll with this trio of traveling magnets. Stitched on perforated plastic, the designs are framed with decorative paper, maps, buttons, and ribbons to create cute magnets that are perfect for motorhomes.

Each design was stitched on a 4" square of White Perforated Plastic (14 ct) and trimmed 8 threads away from design. Three strands of floss were used for Cross Stitch and 1 for Backstitch.

For trims, glue ⅜"w strips of decorative paper and buttons to Designs #1 and #3. Center Design #2 on a 3¾" square of cardboard covered with a road map; add ribbon. Glue a magnet to center back of each design.

Designed by Elaine Porter.

X	DMC	ANC.	COLOR	X	DMC	B'ST	ANC.	COLOR
✱	304	1006	red	V	822		390	beige
◉	400	351	rust	▨	922		1003	orange
◓	646	8581	grey	▣	3346		267	green
–	676	891	lt yellow	△	3348		264	lt green
▦	725	305	yellow		3371	◢	382	brown
◇	783	307	gold					

"SEW" QUICK GIFTS

Cross stitching a present for a fellow needleworker is always a pleasure, especially when the gift expresses a shared love for the same hobby! These clever quips are "sew" quick to fashion that you can count on them even when your time is limited.

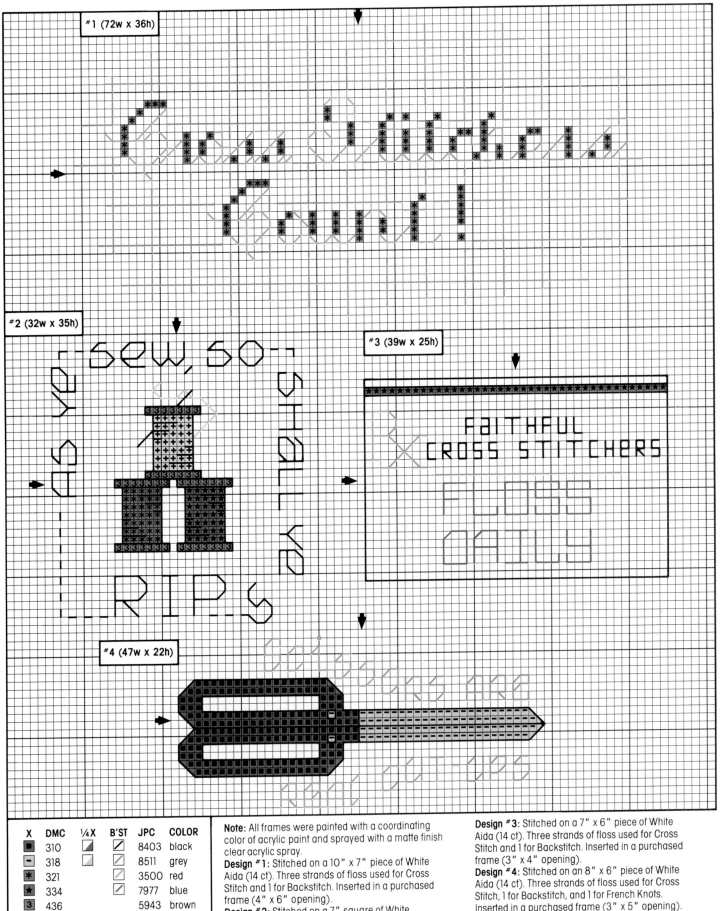

#1 (72w x 36h)

Cross Stitchers Count!

#2 (32w x 35h)

As ye sew, so shall ye RIP!

#3 (39w x 25h)

FAITHFUL
CROSS STITCHERS
FLOSS
ONLY

#4 (47w x 22h)

Scissors are Real Cut-Ups

X	DMC	¼X	B'ST	JPC	COLOR
■	310	◩	◪	8403	black
−	318	◩	◪	8511	grey
*	321		◪	3500	red
★	334		◪	7977	blue
3	436			5943	brown
+	743			2302	yellow
●	321	red French Knot			

* Use 2 strands of floss.

Note: All frames were painted with a coordinating color of acrylic paint and sprayed with a matte finish clear acrylic spray.

Design #1: Stitched on a 10" x 7" piece of White Aida (14 ct). Three strands of floss used for Cross Stitch and 1 for Backstitch. Inserted in a purchased frame (4" x 6" opening).

Design #2: Stitched on a 7" square of White Aida (14 ct). Three strands of floss used for Cross Stitch, 2 for yellow Backstitch, and 1 for black Backstitch. Inserted in a purchased frame (3½" square opening).

Design #3: Stitched on a 7" x 6" piece of White Aida (14 ct). Three strands of floss used for Cross Stitch and 1 for Backstitch. Inserted in a purchased frame (3" x 4" opening).

Design #4: Stitched on an 8" x 6" piece of White Aida (14 ct). Three strands of floss used for Cross Stitch, 1 for Backstitch, and 1 for French Knots. Inserted in a purchased frame (3" x 5" opening).

Designed by Connie Larsen, Needleworks Northwest.

BOOKMARKS FOR GIVING

These pretty page markers make great little gifts to share with your favorite book lovers!

Never underestimate the power of PRAYER

Best friends are a Blest friend

READING IS FUNdamental

X	DMC	¼X	ANC.	COLOR	X	DMC	¼X	B'ST	ANC.	COLOR	X	DMC	¼X	ANC.	COLOR
⟋	ecru		387	ecru	$	745			300	yellow	◆	963		73	lt pink
⊙	210		108	purple	◆	754			1012	peach	▽	3325		129	blue
≡	211		342	lt purple	☆	775	⟋		128	vy lt blue	◇	3716		25	pink
◓	368	⟋	214	green	✖	800	⟋		144	lt blue	Σ	3772		1007	dk flesh
◆	369		1043	lt green	◣	809	◤		130	dk blue	‖	3773		1008	flesh
✳	437		362	tan	★	839		⟋	360	brown	✔	3774		778	lt flesh
✚	712	⟋	926	cream	▢	841			378	taupe					
⊙	738		361	lt tan	♡	842			388	lt taupe					

Each design was stitched on an Ecru Stitch-N-Mark™ Bookmark (18 ct). Two strands of floss used for Cross Stitch and 1 for Backstitch.

Designs by Deborah Lambein.

93

Quick
KITCHEN STITCHIN'

Beautifully decorated bread cloths such as these Four Season Angels, *fanciful fingertip towels, and a montage of mugs and magnets are just a few of the ingredients you'll find in this creative kitchen collection. Like the components of a favorite recipe, these quick-to-whip-up projects can be combined to create tasteful touches to coordinate with your kitchen — and to share with your family and friends. So get stitchin', because it's never been easier to add spice to your kitchen decor!*

95

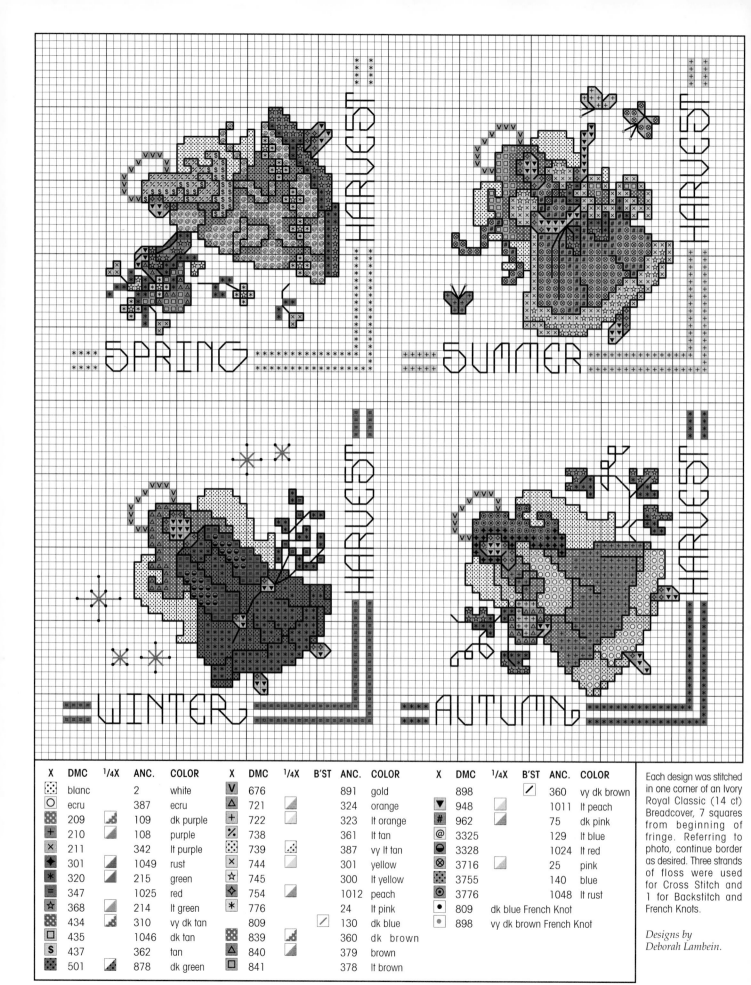

X	DMC	¼X	ANC.	COLOR		X	DMC	¼X	B'ST	ANC.	COLOR		X	DMC	¼X	B'ST	ANC.	COLOR
⊡	blanc		2	white		▽	676			891	gold		▨	898		◢	360	vy dk brown
○	ecru		387	ecru		△	721	◢		324	orange		▼	948	◢		1011	lt peach
▨	209	◢	109	dk purple		+	722	◢		323	lt orange		#	962	◢		75	dk pink
+	210	◢	108	purple		◿	738			361	lt tan		@	3325			129	lt blue
×	211		342	lt purple		⊡	739		⊡	387	vy lt tan		◓	3328			1024	lt red
◆	301		1049	rust		×	744	◢		301	yellow		⊗	3716	◢		25	pink
✳	320	◢	215	green		☆	745			300	lt yellow		▨	3755			140	blue
=	347		1025	red		◈	754			1012	peach		◉	3776			1048	lt rust
☆	368	◢	214	lt green		✳	776			24	lt pink		•	809				dk blue French Knot
▨	434	◢	310	vy dk tan			809		◢	130	dk blue		•	898				vy dk brown French Knot
□	435		1046	dk tan		▨	839		◢	360	dk brown							
S	437		362	tan		△	840		◢	379	brown							
▨	501	◢	878	dk green		□	841			378	lt brown							

Each design was stitched in one corner of an Ivory Royal Classic (14 ct) Breadcover, 7 squares from beginning of fringe. Referring to photo, continue border as desired. Three strands of floss were used for Cross Stitch and 1 for Backstitch and French Knots.

Designs by Deborah Lambein.

FINGERTIP BASKETS

Welcome a new neighbor with our quick-to-stitch fingertip towels. Embellished with baskets of fruit and flowers, they'll make ideal housewarming gifts for the kitchen.

X	DMC	ANC.	COLOR
V	209	109	purple
▲	320	215	green
3	434	310	brown
C	472	253	yellow green
S	722	323	orange
−	744	301	yellow
◒	3328	1024	rose

Each design stitched on the White Aida (14 ct) insert of a fingertip towel. Three strands of floss used for Cross Stitch.

Designed by Deborah Lambein.

55w x 26h

53w x 20h

These quick-to-stitch mugs are adorned with sweet renditions of the fresh fruit we enjoy in the summer.

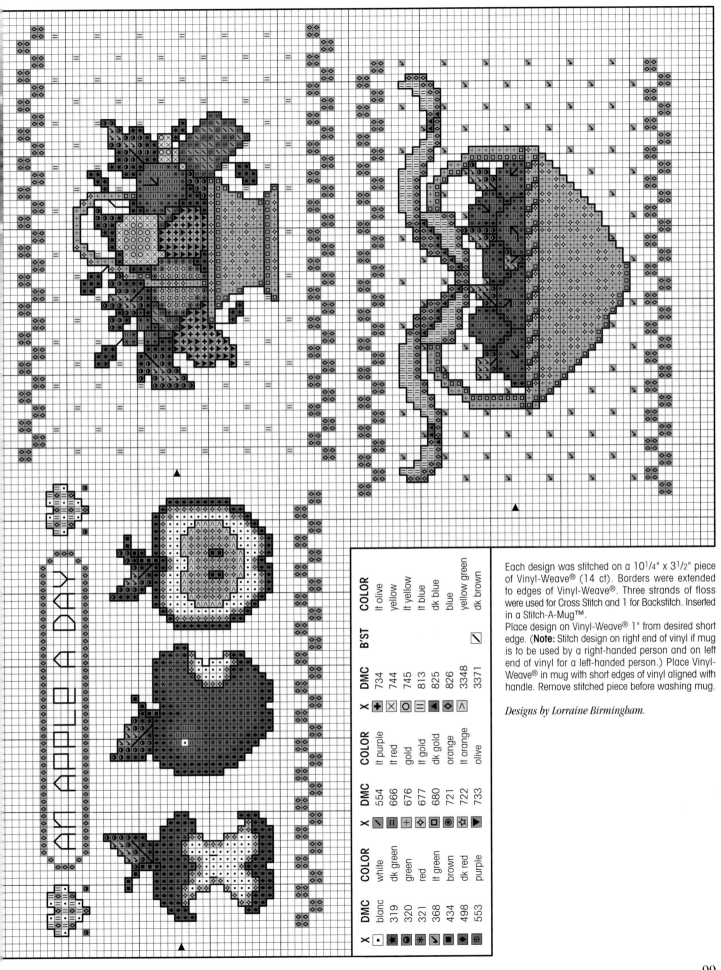

Each design was stitched on a 10¹/₄" x 3¹/₂" piece of Vinyl-Weave® (14 ct). Borders were extended to edges of Vinyl-Weave®. Three strands of floss were used for Cross Stitch and 1 for Backstitch. Inserted in a Stitch-A-Mug™.
Place design on Vinyl-Weave® 1" from desired short edge. (**Note:** Stitch design on right end of vinyl if mug is to be used by a right-handed person and on left end of vinyl for a left-handed person.) Place Vinyl-Weave® in mug with short edges of vinyl aligned with handle. Remove stitched piece before washing mug.

Designs by Lorraine Birmingham.

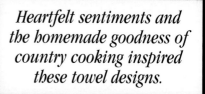

Heartfelt sentiments and the homemade goodness of country cooking inspired these towel designs.

X	DMC	1/4X	B'ST	COLOR
	blanc			white
	300	◪		dk rust
	301	◪		lt rust
	321	◪		red
	415			lt grey
	433			brown
	434	◪	◩	lt brown
	435	◪		dk tan
	436	◪		tan
	437			lt tan
	498			dk red
	552	◪		dk purple
	553	◪		purple
	554			lt purple
	645			grey
	647			dk grey
	666			lt red
	676	◪		gold
	677	◪		lt gold
	680	◪		dk gold
	732	◪		dk yellow green
	733	◪		yellow green
	734	◪		lt yellow green
	738			vy lt tan
	762	◪		vy lt grey
	825	◪		dk blue
	826			blue
	839			taupe
	975	◪		rust
	3347	◪		green
	3348	◪		lt green
	3371		◩	brown black
	3687	◪		rose
	3688			lt rose
	3776	◪		vy lt rose
	3371			dk brown Fr. Knot

h design was stitched on an Ecru Park Avenue
ertip™ Towel with 14 ct insert. Three strands
oss were used for Cross Stitch and 1 for all
r stitches.

igns by Lorraine Birmingham.

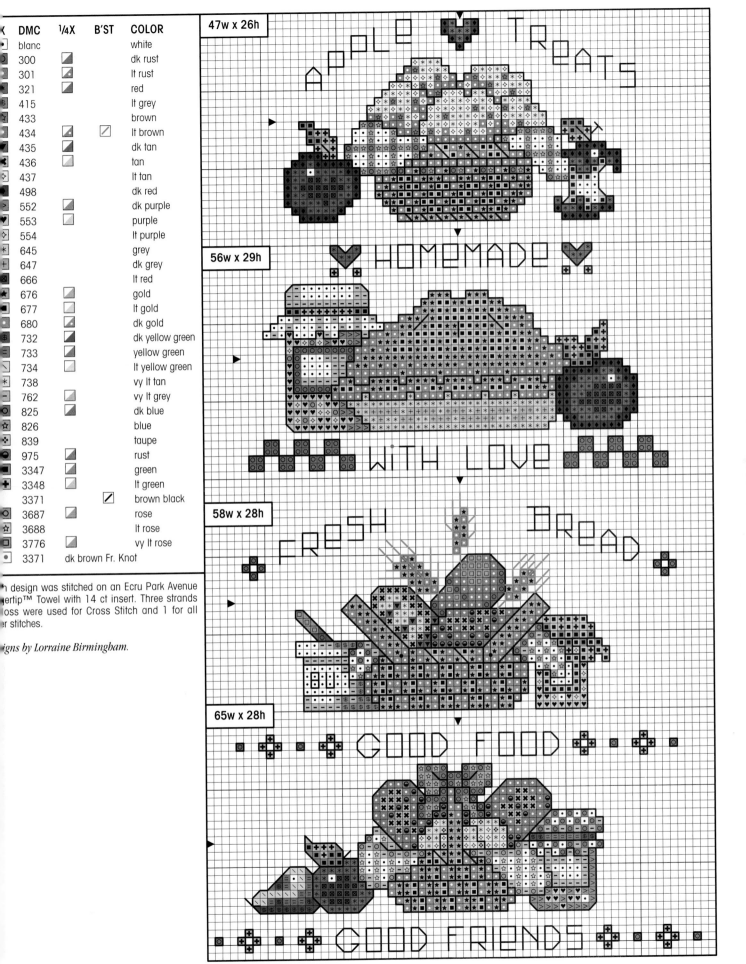

Add country charm to your kitchen with these homespun magnet designs! Designed for two sizes of acrylic magnets, they're great for displaying snapshots, "to-do" lists, or your child's artwork.

X	DMC	B'ST	ANC.	COLOR
	blanc		2	white
⊙	301		1049	vy dk orange
▦	310	╱	403	black
	311	╱	148	vy dk blue
✚	318		399	grey
▨	319		218	vy dk green
◇	320		215	green
▨	322		978	dk blue
▬	334		977	blue
✳	347		1025	red
8	367		217	dk green
☆	368		214	lt green
4	369		1043	vy lt green
⊖	402		1047	orange
▲	413		401	dk grey
S	434		310	vy dk tan
X	435		1046	dk tan
V	437		362	tan
▦	471		266	yellow green
⊙	472		253	lt yellow green
N	642		392	dk beige
△	644		830	beige
★	676		891	gold
H	677		886	lt gold
✚	729		890	dk gold
C	738		361	lt tan
−	744		301	yellow
▲	746		276	vy lt yellow
◎	760		1022	mauve
✦	776		24	lt pink
◇	800		144	lt purple blue
◻	809		130	purple blue
✳	822		390	lt beige
▨	840		379	lt brown
☆	842		388	vy lt brown
4	898	╱	360	brown
▨	948		1011	peach
⊖	962		75	dk pink
⊙	3072		847	lt grey
S	3325		129	vy lt blue
X	3328		1024	dk mauve
V	3716		25	pink
◆	3755		140	lt blue
⊙	3756		1037	baby blue
✦	3776		1048	dk orange
•	898			brown French Knot

Designs #2, #4, and **#6** were each stitched on a 2¼"dia. circle of Vinyl-Weave™ (14 ct). **Designs #1, #3,** and **#5** were each stitched on a 2⅝"dia. circle of Vinyl-Weave™ (14 ct). Three strands of floss were used for Cross Stitch and 1 for Backstitch and French Knots. **Designs #2, #4,** and **#6** were each inserted in a small Stitch-a-Magnet™. **Designs #1, #3,** and **#5** were each inserted in a large Stitch-a-Magnet™.

Designed by Deborah Lambein.

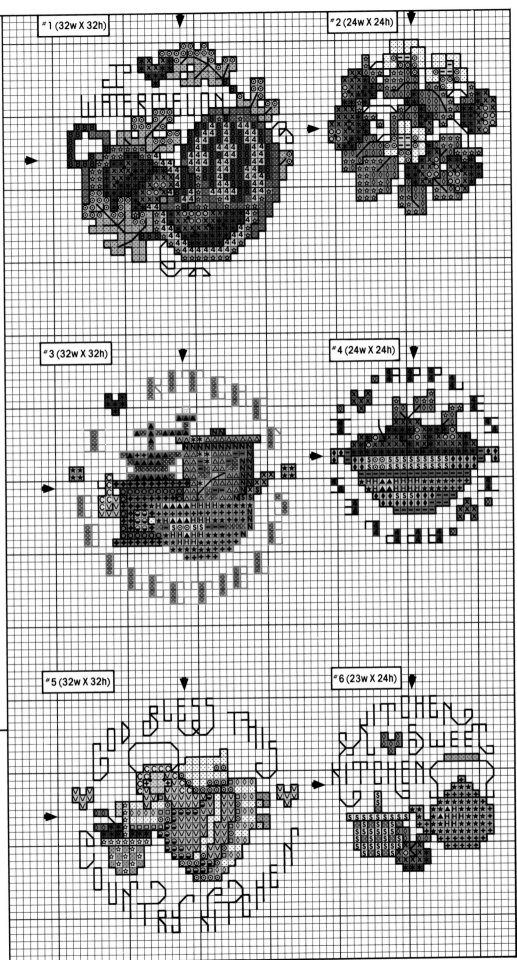

HARVEST BREAD COVERS

Accented with an autumn-rich harvest of squash, corn, and apples, our bread covers will add the perfect touch to your Thanksgiving table. Quick to stitch, they'll also make wonderful gifts to leave behind for the hostess of a holiday potluck.

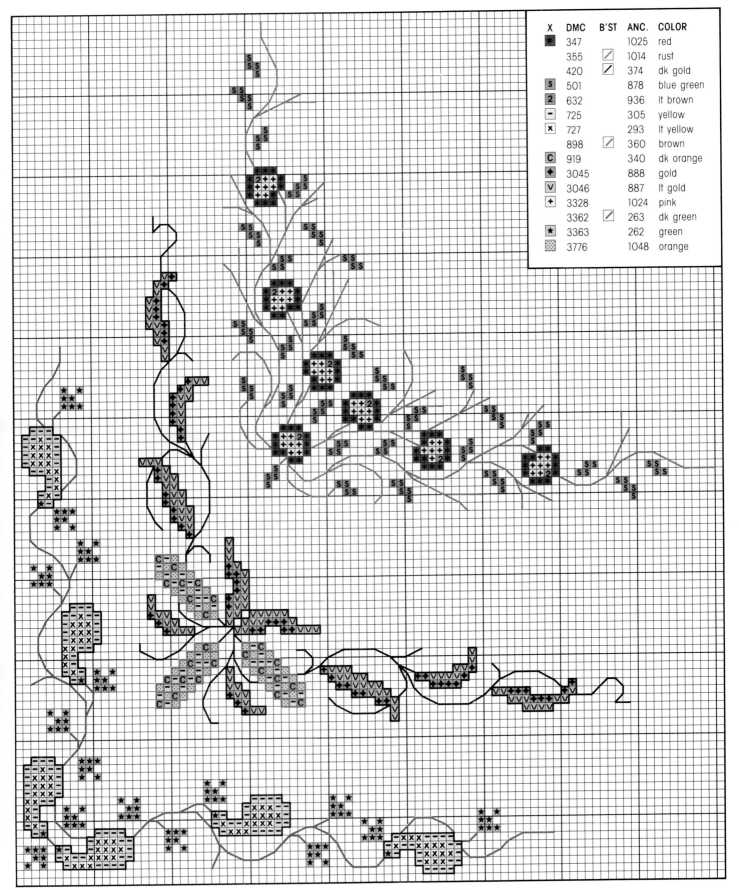

X	DMC	B'ST	ANC.	COLOR
✳	347		1025	red
	355	╱	1014	rust
	420	╱	374	dk gold
S	501		878	blue green
2	632		936	lt brown
–	725		305	yellow
✕	727		293	lt yellow
	898	╱	360	brown
C	919		340	dk orange
✦	3045		888	gold
V	3046		887	lt gold
+	3328		1024	pink
	3362	╱	263	dk green
★	3363		262	green
▧	3776		1048	orange

Each design stitched on one corner of an Oatmeal Soft Touch™ (14 ct) Breadcover 7 threads from beginning of fringe. Three strands of floss used for Cross Stitch and 1 for Backstitch.

Designs by Jane Chandler.

GARDEN FRESH

Adorning a wreath or posing as plant pokes, these mini pillows celebrate summer's fresh vegetables.

Broccoli

Radish

Eggplant

Carrots

Corn

Tomato

106

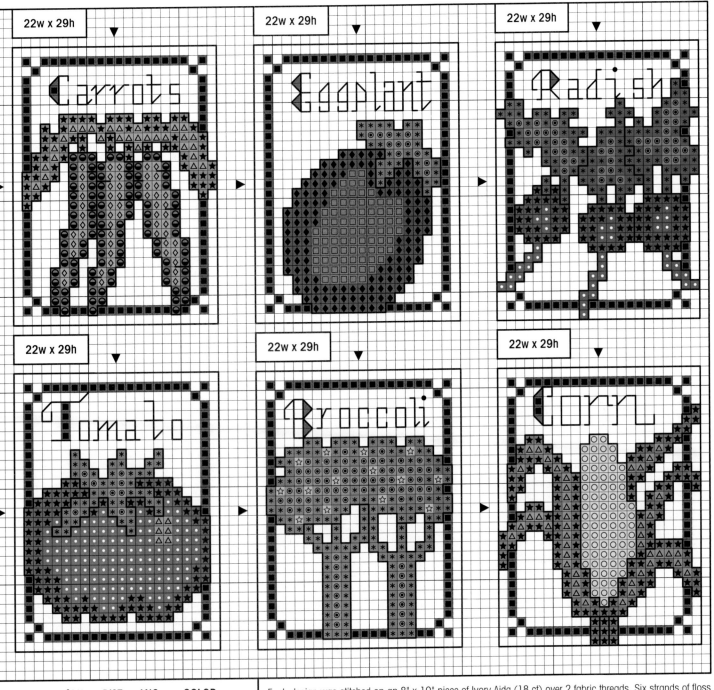

X	DMC	1/4X	B'ST	ANC.	COLOR
★	321			9046	dk red
△	352			9	lt red
◆	550			102	dk purple
□	552			99	purple
▪	666			46	red
◕	720			326	orange
◇	721			324	lt orange
○	725			305	yellow
■	938	◢	╱	381	brown
✳	987			244	dk green
◉	988			243	green
☆	989			242	lt green
★	3346			267	yellow green
△	3347			266	lt yellow green
●	938			381	brown Fr. knot

Each design was stitched on an 8" x 10" piece of Ivory Aida (18 ct) over 2 fabric threads. Six strands of floss were used for Cross Stitch and 2 for all other stitches. Made into mini pillows.

For each mini pillow, trim stitched piece to desired size plus 1/2" on all sides. Cut backing fabric (same fabric as stitched piece) same size as stitched piece. Matching wrong sides and raw edges, machine stitch fabric pieces together 1/2" from bottom and side edges. Stuff pillow with polyester fiberfill; machine stitch across top of pillow 1/2" from edges. Fringe fabric to one square from machine-stitched lines.

Designs by Polly Carbonari.

107

You don't have to wait for April showers to bring May flowers with our beautiful floral mugs. The vibrant blossoms will brighten any day, rain or shine.

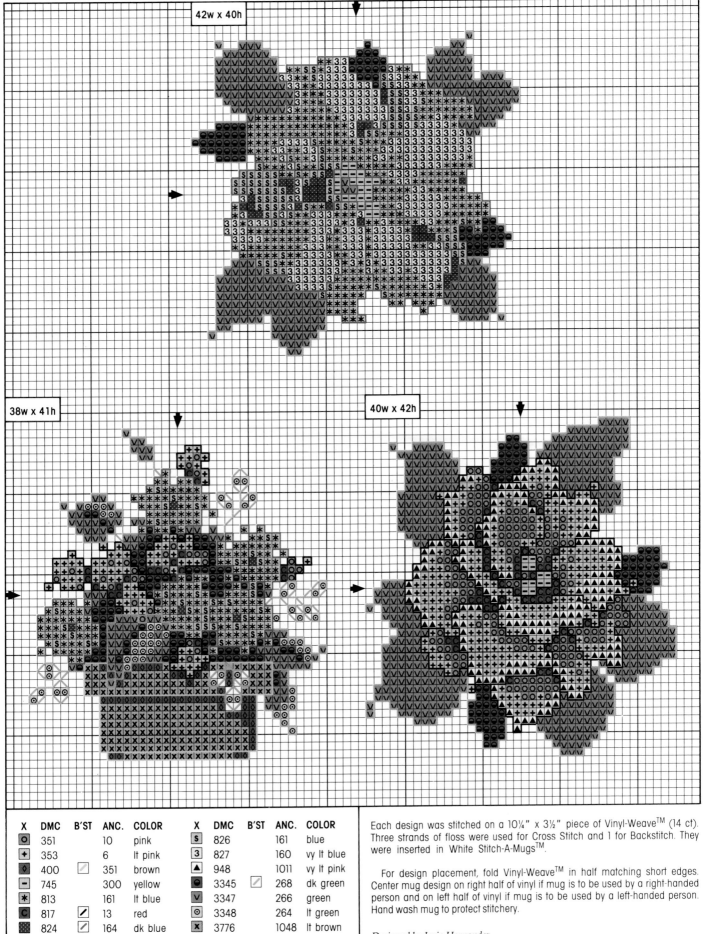

X	DMC	B'ST	ANC.	COLOR	X	DMC	B'ST	ANC.	COLOR
⊙	351		10	pink	S	826		161	blue
+	353		6	lt pink	3	827		160	vy lt blue
◆	400	╱	351	brown	▲	948		1011	vy lt pink
−	745		300	yellow	◉	3345		268	dk green
*	813		161	lt blue	V	3347		266	green
C	817	╱	13	red	⊙	3348		264	lt green
▦	824	╱	164	dk blue	X	3776		1048	lt brown

Each design was stitched on a 10¼" x 3½" piece of Vinyl-Weave™ (14 ct). Three strands of floss were used for Cross Stitch and 1 for Backstitch. They were inserted in White Stitch-A-Mugs™.

For design placement, fold Vinyl-Weave™ in half matching short edges. Center mug design on right half of vinyl if mug is to be used by a right-handed person and on left half of vinyl if mug is to be used by a left-handed person. Hand wash mug to protect stitchery.

Designed by Jorja Hernandez,
Kooler Design Studio.

COUNTRY KITCHEN WELCOME

It'll be a snap to treat a friend to a special lunch with our quick and delicious Mexican quiche. Along with this flavorful recipe for two, there's a delightful design for a cute country fingertip towel. Accented with barnyard pals, it will make her feel welcome in your roost, and add a homey touch to your kitchen decor, too.

MEXICAN QUICHE FOR TWO

1 8½-inch flour tortilla
½ cup shredded Monterey Jack cheese
½ to ¾ cup half and half
3 eggs
¼ teaspoon salt
⅛ teaspoon ground black pepper
½ pound chorizo sausage
2 small green onions, sliced

Sour cream and fresh cilantro to garnish

Preheat oven to 350 degrees. Wrap tortilla in microwave-safe plastic wrap; microwave 10 seconds to soften. Place tortilla in a greased 3 to 4-cup baking dish with about a 5-inch diameter bottom. Sprinkle cheese over tortilla. In a small bowl, whisk half and half, eggs, salt, and pepper; pour over cheese. Bake 35 to 40 minutes or until eggs are set.
While quiche is baking, prepare sausage mixture. In a heavy medium skillet over medium-high heat, cook sausage until lightly browned; drain. Stirring occasionally, add green onions and cook 2 minutes longer. Spoon sausage mixture over hot quiche. Garnish with sour cream and fresh cilantro. Serve warm.
Yield: 2 servings

X	DMC	¼X	B'ST	COLOR
◕	347	◪		red
✳	433			brown
	898		◩	dk brown
△	920			rust
✕	922			lt rust
◇	3033			beige
▨	3046	◪		gold
−	3047	◪		lt gold
V	3782			khaki
•	898			dk brown French Knot

WELCOME (62w x 30h)

Designed by Deborah Lambein.

The design was stitched on the Tea-Dyed Aida (14 ct) insert of a velour fingertip towel. Three strands of floss were used for Cross Stitch and 1 for Backstitch and French Knots.

110

Brighten the buffet at your next get-together with these two sunny surprises! The pretty basket cloth blooms with golden sunflowers to add a touch of warmth to the table, and our Sunflower Cheese Ball is a fun treat.

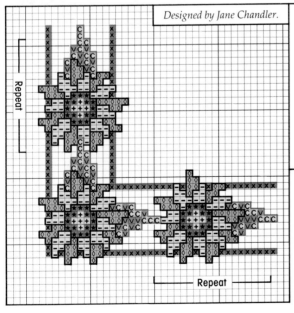

Designed by Jane Chandler.

X	DMC	B'ST	JPC	COLOR
✖	311		7980	blue
✚	434		5000	lt brown
✔	469		6261	green
Ⅽ	471		6010	lt green
−	725		2298	yellow
◊	783		5307	dk yellow
★	801		5475	dk brown
	936	╱	6269	dk green
	975	╱	5349	brown

The design was stitched on a Country Oatmeal Royal Classic Breadcover (14 ct). Three strands of floss were used for Cross Stitch and 1 for Backstitch. The design was stitched in one corner of bread cover, ½" from beginning of fringe. Repeat design as desired.

SUNFLOWER CHEESE BALL

1½ cups lightly salted roasted sunflower kernels, divided
1 package (8 ounces) cream cheese, softened
3 ounces blue cheese, crumbled
¼ cup finely chopped celery
¼ cup finely chopped green onions
2 tablespoons sour cream
1 teaspoon instant chicken bouillon granules
⅛ teaspoon ground red pepper
1 bag (15 ounces) nacho cheese tortilla chips

In a medium bowl, combine 1 cup sunflower kernels and next 7 ingredients. Shape into a ball and coat with remaining ½ cup sunflower kernels. Wrap in plastic wrap, and refrigerate 8 hours or overnight to allow flavors to blend.

To serve, let stand at room temperature 20 to 30 minutes to soften. Press tortilla chips into sides of cheese ball to resemble flower petals. Serve with additional chips.
Yield: 1 cheese ball

A harvest of herbs holds the promise of flavorful foods and fancy garnishes. Whether fresh-cut or hung to dry, the delicate leaves and blooms are as delightful to the eye as their flavors are to the palate. In these designs, we capture eight flowering herbs at the peak of their beauty. What a natural way for them to live forever!

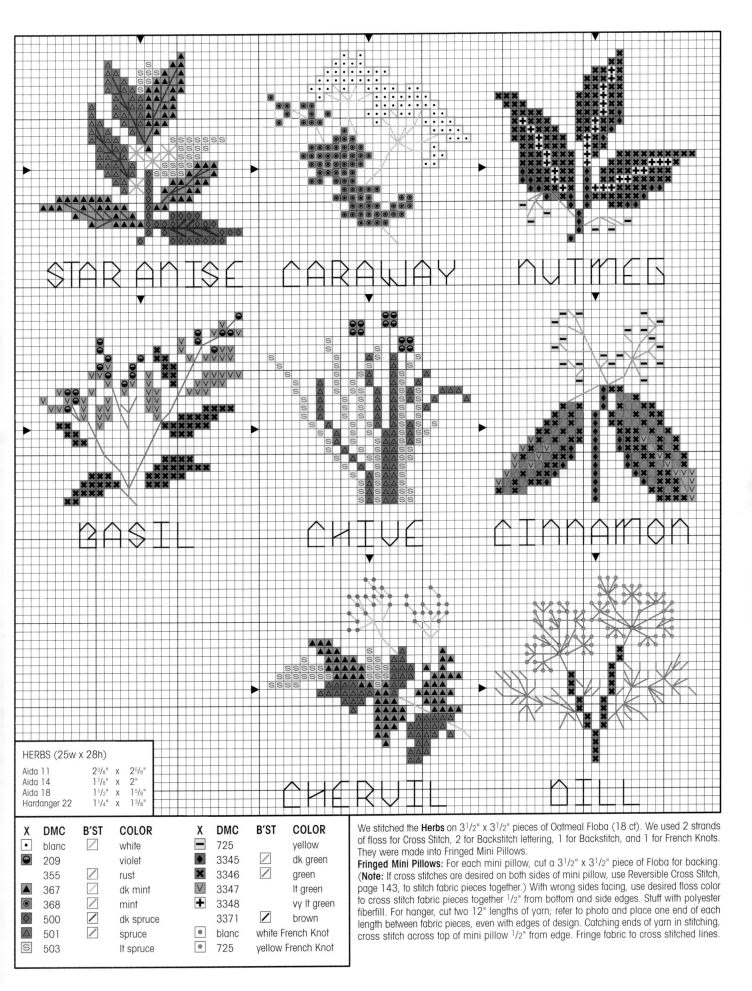

STAR ANISE

CARAWAY

NUTMEG

BASIL

CHIVE

CINNAMON

HERBS (25w x 28h)

Aida 11	2³/₈" x 2⁵/₈"
Aida 14	1⁷/₈" x 2"
Aida 18	1¹/₂" x 1⁵/₈"
Hardanger 22	1¹/₄" x 1³/₈"

CHERVIL

DILL

We stitched the **Herbs** on 3¹/₂" x 3¹/₂" pieces of Oatmeal Floba (18 ct). We used 2 strands of floss for Cross Stitch, 2 for Backstitch lettering, 1 for Backstitch, and 1 for French Knots. They were made into Fringed Mini Pillows.

Fringed Mini Pillows: For each mini pillow, cut a 3¹/₂" x 3¹/₂" piece of Floba for backing. (Note: If cross stitches are desired on both sides of mini pillow, use Reversible Cross Stitch, page 143, to stitch fabric pieces together.) With wrong sides facing, use desired floss color to cross stitch fabric pieces together ¹/₂" from bottom and side edges. Stuff with polyester fiberfill. For hanger, cut two 12" lengths of yarn; refer to photo and place one end of each length between fabric pieces, even with edges of design. Catching ends of yarn in stitching, cross stitch across top of mini pillow ¹/₂" from edge. Fringe fabric to cross stitched lines.

X	DMC	B'ST	COLOR	X	DMC	B'ST	COLOR
▪	blanc	╱	white	▬	725		yellow
◕	209		violet	◆	3345	╱	dk green
	355	╱	rust	✖	3346	╱	green
▲	367	╱	dk mint	✔	3347		lt green
⊙	368	╱	mint	✛	3348		vy lt green
◈	500	╱	dk spruce		3371		brown
△	501	╱	spruce	●	blanc	╱	white French Knot
S	503		lt spruce	●	725		yellow French Knot

113

"UDDERLY" DELICIOUS

Cross stitched with country cows and a checkered border, our bovine bread cloth is "udderly" delightful! It'll make a charming accompaniment to a snack of our tasty Malted Milk Cookies and a tall glass of milk.

The design was stitched in one corner of an 18" square of Ivory Aida (14 ct) with design 1" from raw edge. Three strands of floss were used for Cross Stitch and 1 for Backstitch.

For bread cover, machine stitch 7 squares from raw edge on all sides; fringe fabric to machine-stitched lines.

Design by Deborah Lambein.

MALTED MILK COOKIES

- ²/₃ cup butter or margarine, softened
- ¹/₂ cup sifted confectioners sugar
- 2¹/₄ cups all-purpose flour
- ¹/₂ cup malted milk mix
- ³/₄ cup crushed malted milk ball candies
- 1 teaspoon vanilla extract
- 1 package (11.5 ounces) milk chocolate chips

In a large bowl, cream butter and confectioners sugar. In a medium bowl, combine flour, malted milk mix, and crushed candies. Add dry ingredients and vanilla to creamed mixture; blend (mixture will be crumbly). Pressing firmly, shape dough into 1-inch balls and place on ungreased baking sheets; chill 15 minutes.

Preheat oven to 350 degrees. Bake 12 to 15 minutes or until lightly browned. Transfer cookies to a wire rack to cool.

Stirring frequently, melt chocolate chips in a heavy medium saucepan over low heat; remove from heat. Placing each cookie on a fork and holding over saucepan, spoon chocolate over cookies. Place on a wire rack with waxed paper underneath. Allow chocolate to harden. Store in an airtight container in a cool place.
Yield: about 4 dozen cookies

X	DMC	¹/₄X	B'ST	ANC.	COLOR
⊡	blanc	⊡		2	white
▨	310	◪	╱	403	black
▲	334	◩		977	blue
▤	347			1025	red
◉	353			6	peach
★	676	◪		891	gold
	898		╱	360	brown

In a word, this little shelf scarf is a blessing! Featuring jars of colorful jelly topped with homespun cloths, the design offers a pantry prayer that's sure to brighten your kitchen.

Bless This Pantry was stitched on an Ivory Royal Classic Bread Cover (14 ct). The design was stitched over 2 fabric threads. Six strands of floss were used for Cross Stitch, 3 for dk blue Backstitch, and 2 for all other Backstitch and Lazy Daisies. The design was centered with bottom edge of design 1" from beginning of fringe. See Pantry Scarf Finishing, page 144.

Design by Connie Larsen, Needleworks, Northwest.

BLESS THIS PANTRY (89w x 28h)

X	DMC	¼X	B'ST	JPC	COLOR	X	DMC	¼X	B'ST	JPC	COLOR
◇	ecru			1002	ecru	+	932			7050	lt blue
⊙	327			4101	purple		3371		∕	5478	brown
✕	680			2876	gold	★	3750		∕		dk blue
⊖	816			3410	red	∅	3371		brown Lazy Daisy		
✳	930			7052	blue						

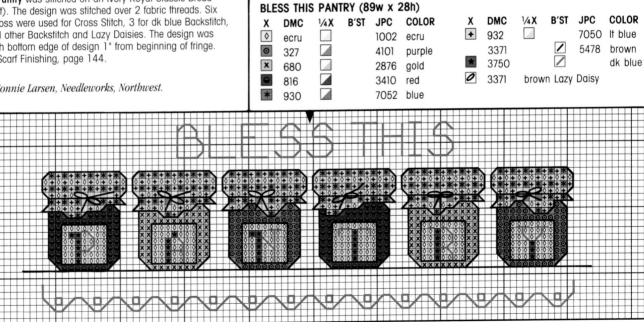

BERRY SAMPLER

Delectable berries gathered fresh from the vine for preserving or serving are one of the sweet pleasures of warm weather. Stitched separately or together, our motifs serve up a sampling of these favorite fruits.

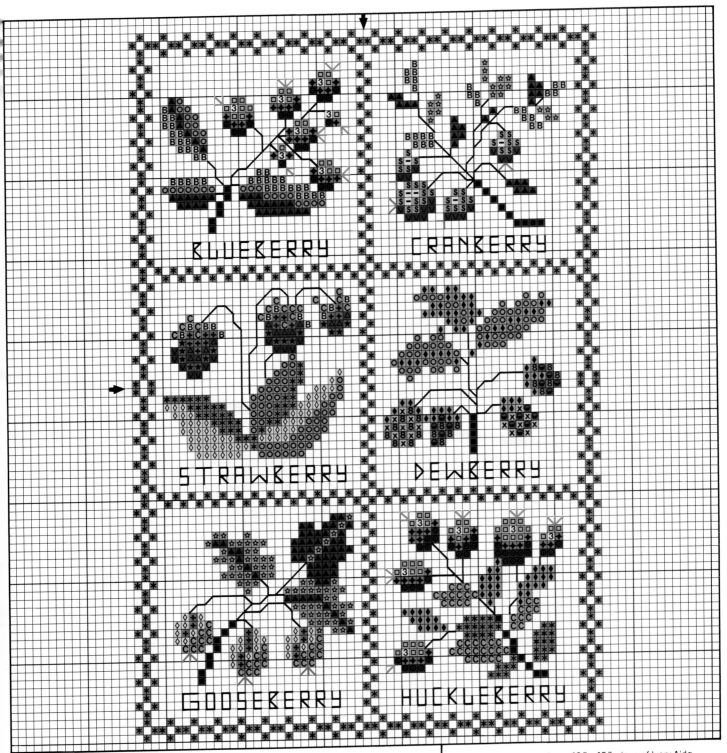

Berry Sampler: Stitched on a 13" x 15" piece of Ivory Aida (14 ct). Three strands of floss used for Cross Stitch and 1 for Backstitch. Custom framed.

Jar Lids: Blueberry and **Gooseberry** each stitched separately on 7" squares of Ivory Aida (14 ct). Three strands of floss used for Cross Stitch and 1 for Backstitch. Inserted in wide mouth jar lids.

For jar lid, use **outer edge** of jar lid for pattern and draw a circle on adhesive mounting board. Cutting slightly inside drawn line, cut out circle. Using **opening** of jar lid for pattern, cut a circle of batting. Center batting on adhesive side of board and press in place. Center stitched piece on batting and press edges onto adhesive board; trim edges close to board. Glue board inside jar lid. (**Note:** A mason jar puff-up kit may also be used to finish jar lid.)

Designed by Barbara Christopher.

The fruits of Mother Nature abound in this collection of bountiful bread cloths. The plentiful designs work up quickly, so you'll have time to "harvest" them all!

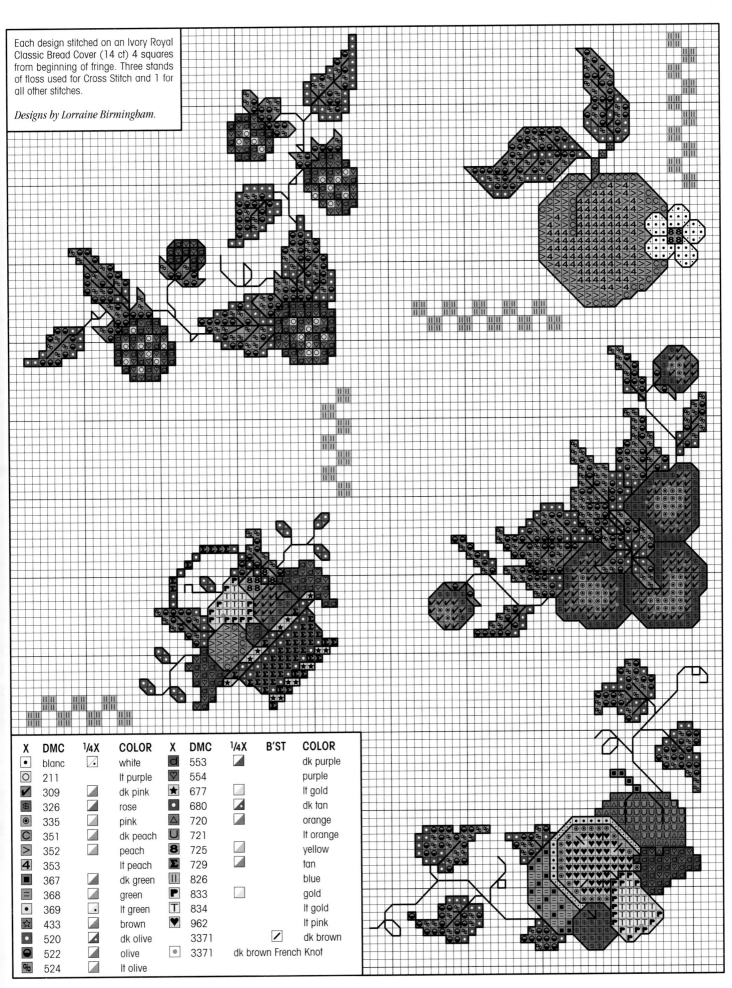

Each design stitched on an Ivory Royal Classic Bread Cover (14 ct) 4 squares from beginning of fringe. Three stands of floss used for Cross Stitch and 1 for all other stitches.

Designs by Lorraine Birmingham.

X	DMC	¼X	COLOR	X	DMC	¼X	B'ST	COLOR
•	blanc		white		553			dk purple
O	211		lt purple		554			purple
	309		dk pink	★	677			lt gold
$	326		rose		680			dk tan
⊙	335		pink	△	720			orange
C	351		dk peach	U	721			lt orange
>	352		peach	8	725			yellow
4	353		lt peach	Σ	729			tan
■	367		dk green	‖	826			blue
=	368		green	P	833			gold
•	369		lt green	T	834			lt gold
☆	433		brown	♥	962			lt pink
◘	520		dk olive		3371		◢	dk brown
●	522		olive	⊙	3371			dk brown French Knot
%	524		lt olive					

Fast
FASHION FLAIR

Adding your handiwork to ready-to-wear clothing is a great way to show off your personal style and create fun fashions. With this versatile assortment of designs, you can spruce up apparel for the whole family — from newborns to adults — in a flash! You'll create a bounty of Garden-Fresh Fashions like these with eye-catching fruit, vegetable, and flower designs, as well as sweet tees for baby, pretty sweaters for Mom, some kid-friendly tops, and a sweatshirt for a Dad who loves sailing.

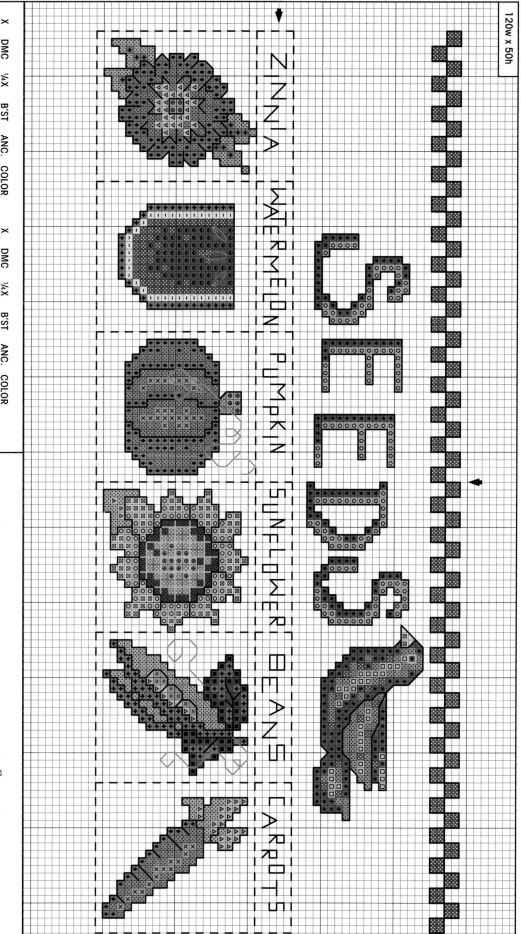

X	DMC	¼X	B'ST	ANC.	COLOR
	ecru			387	ecru
	304			1006	dk red
	310			403	black
	347			1025	red
	433			358	brown
	434			310	lt brown
	471			266	lt green
	472			253	vy lt green
	645			273	grey
	720			326	dk orange
	721			324	orange
	722			323	lt orange

X	DMC	¼X	B'ST	ANC.	COLOR
	725			305	dk yellow
	726			295	yellow
	741			304	yellow orange
	801			359	dk brown
	844			1041	dk grey
	895			1044	vy dk green
	930			1035	dk blue
	3345			268	dk green
	3346			267	green
	3750			1036	dk blue
	310				black Lazy Daisy Stitch

120w x 50h

ZINNIA WATERMELON PUMPKIN SUNFLOWER BEANS CARROTS

Note: For waste canvas projects, see Working on Waste Canvas, page 143.

T-Shirt: The entire design was stitched over an 18" x 10" piece of 10 mesh waste canvas on a purchased T-shirt. Four strands of floss were used for Cross Stitch and 2 for Backstitch and Lazy Daisy Stitches. The design was centered horizontally 2" from bottom of neckband.

T-Shirt: Seed Packets only were each stitched over a 3½" x 4" piece of 8.5 mesh waste canvas on a purchased T-shirt. Refer to photo (pages 120-121) for placement of designs. Six strands of floss were used for Cross Stitch and 2 for Backstitch and Lazy Daisy Stitches.

Chambray Shirt: Sunflower packet only was stitched over a 3½" x 4" piece of 8.5 mesh waste canvas on the pocket of a purchased shirt. Six strands of floss were used for Cross Stitch and 2 for Backstitch.

Pin: Crow only was stitched on a 5" square of Antique White Aida (11 ct). Four strands of floss were used for Cross Stitch and 2 for Backstitch. It was stiffened and a pin back was glued to center back of stitched piece. To stiffen stitched piece, apply a heavy coat of fabric stiffener to back of stitched piece using a small foam brush. Cut one piece of medium weight fabric same size as stitched piece for backing. Matching wrong sides, place stitched piece on backing fabric, smoothing stitched piece while pressing fabrics together; allow to dry. Apply fabric stiffener to backing fabric; allow to dry. Referring to photo (pages 120-121), trim stitched piece close to edges of design.

Design by Susan Fouts.
Needlework adaptation by Christine Street.

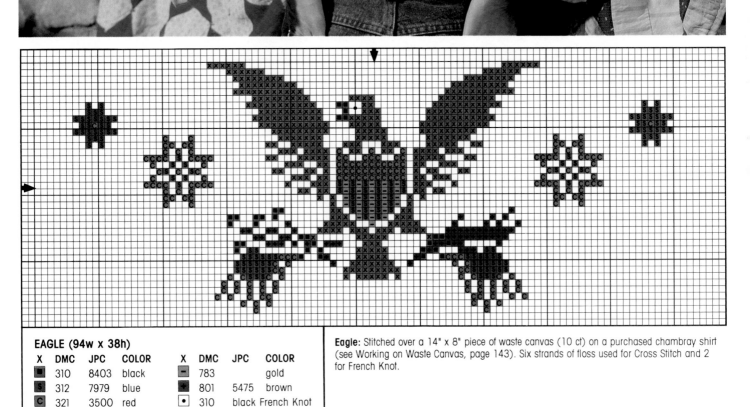

A GREAT AMERICAN SHIRT

Inspired by Early American sampler motifs, our eagle design adds patriotic spirit to a chambray shirt. It's a great way to show your love of country.

EAGLE (94w x 38h)

X	DMC	JPC	COLOR		X	DMC	JPC	COLOR
■	310	8403	black		−	783		gold
S	312	7979	blue		✳	801	5475	brown
C	321	3500	red		•	310		black French Knot
X	434	5000	lt brown					

Eagle: Stitched over a 14" x 8" piece of waste canvas (10 ct) on a purchased chambray shirt (see Working on Waste Canvas, page 143). Six strands of floss used for Cross Stitch and 2 for French Knot.

Whether you receive them from a sweetheart or as a gift for Mother's Day, corsages help mark the memorable events in your life. These lovely gardenia corsages for sweaters will make you feel like any day is a special occasion.

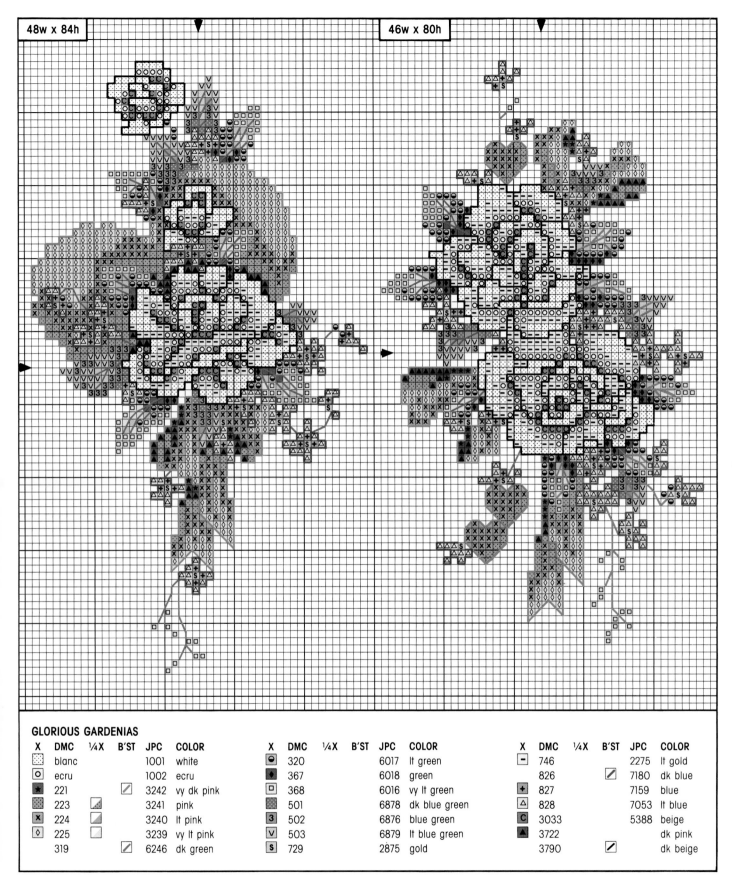

| 48w x 84h | | | | | 46w x 80h | | | | |

GLORIOUS GARDENIAS

X	DMC	¼X	B'ST	JPC	COLOR	X	DMC	¼X	B'ST	JPC	COLOR	X	DMC	¼X	B'ST	JPC	COLOR
	blanc			1001	white	◕	320			6017	lt green	−	746			2275	lt gold
○	ecru			1002	ecru	◆	367			6018	green		826		/	7180	dk blue
★	221		/	3242	vy dk pink	▢	368			6016	vy lt green	✚	827			7159	blue
▨	223	◩		3241	pink	▨	501			6878	dk blue green	△	828			7053	lt blue
✗	224	◪		3240	lt pink	3	502			6876	blue green	C	3033			5388	beige
◇	225	◻		3239	vy lt pink	V	503			6879	lt blue green	▲	3722				dk pink
	319		/	6246	dk green	S	729			2875	gold		3790		/		dk beige

Glorious Gardenias were each stitched over an 8" x 11" piece of 12 mesh waste canvas on a purchased sweater. Three strands of floss were used for Cross Stitch and 1 for Backstitch. See Working on Waste Canvas, page 143.

Designs by Mary Vincent Bertrand.

You'll be sure to spot some smiles when you wear this T-shirt sporting our comical cowpoke cottontail. The bovine bunny is quick to finish because only the colored portions of the design are stitched!

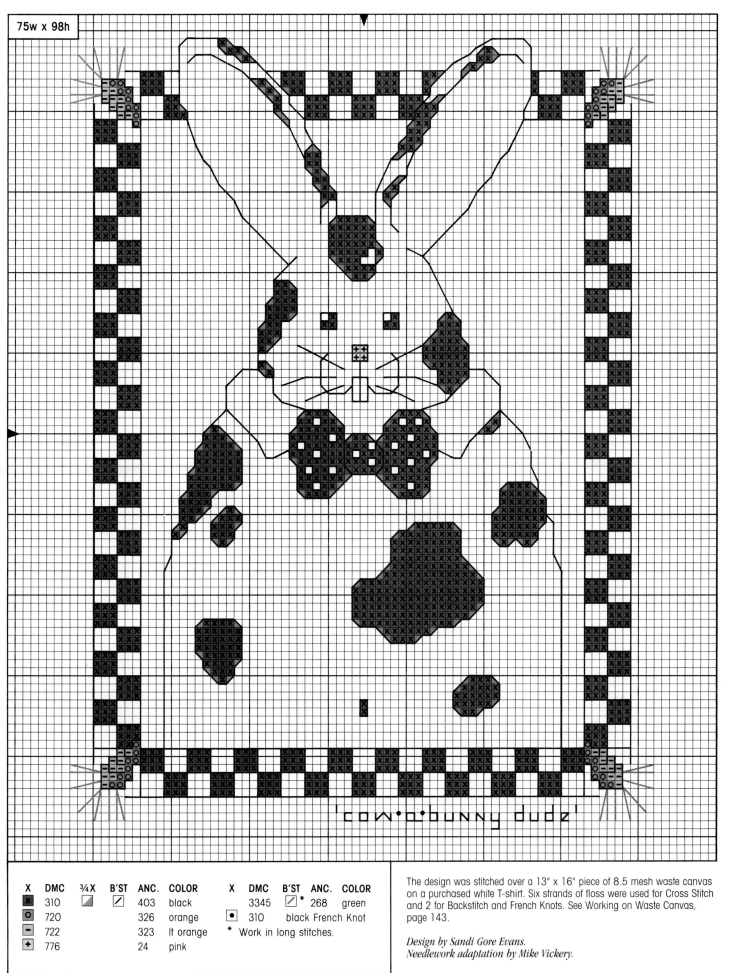

'cow·a·bunny dude'

X	DMC	¾X	B'ST	ANC.	COLOR	X	DMC	B'ST	ANC.	COLOR
■	310	◪	◪	403	black		3345	◪*	268	green
◉	720			326	orange	●	310			black French Knot
▬	722			323	lt orange	*	Work in long stitches.			
✛	776			24	pink					

75w x 98h

The design was stitched over a 13" x 16" piece of 8.5 mesh waste canvas on a purchased white T-shirt. Six strands of floss were used for Cross Stitch and 2 for Backstitch and French Knots. See Working on Waste Canvas, page 143.

Design by Sandi Gore Evans.
Needlework adaptation by Mike Vickery.

127

NIGH-NIGH

These sweet tees are tops for baby! The precious
cover-ups sport a bevy of playful bunnies and kittens.
What a fun way to dress up a newborn's wardrobe!

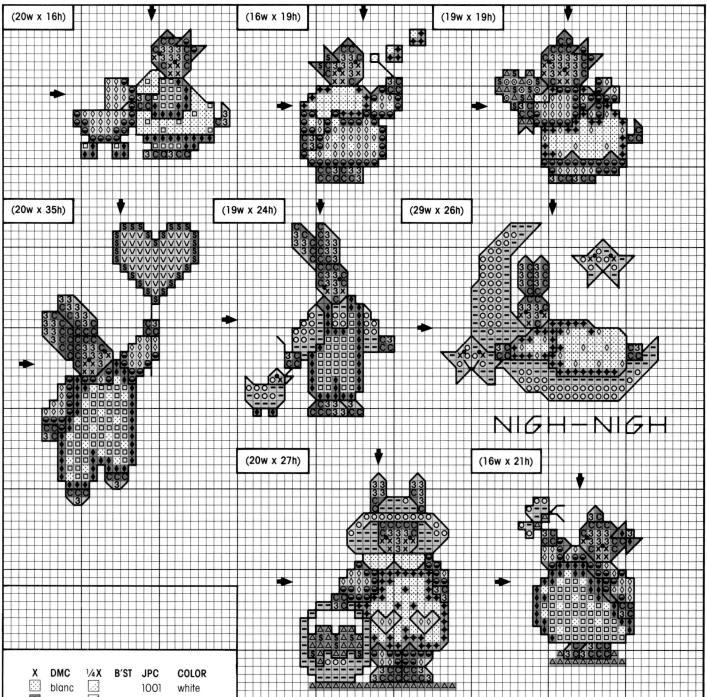

X	DMC	¼X	B'ST	JPC	COLOR
	blanc			1001	white
S	210			4303	violet
V	211			4303	lt violet
X	353			3006	peach
△	563			6210	green
⊙	564			6209	lt green
C	738			5375	tan
3	739			5369	lt tan
−	744			2293	yellow
O	745			2296	lt yellow
◆	762			8510	grey
◇	776			3281	lt pink
◆	813			7161	blue
□	827			7159	lt blue
◨	3326			3126	pink
	3371		╱	5478	brown
•	3371			brown French Knot	

Note: For projects, the designs were stitched over 14 mesh waste canvas on purchased T-shirts. Three strands of floss were used for Cross Stitch, 1 for Backstitch, and 1 for French Knots.

WORKING ON WASTE CANVAS

Waste canvas is a special canvas that provides an evenweave grid for placing stitches on fabric. After the design is worked over the canvas, the canvas threads are removed, leaving the design on the fabric. The canvas is available in several mesh sizes.

Cut waste canvas 1" larger than design size on all sides; cover edges of canvas with masking tape. Cut a piece of lightweight, nonfusible interfacing the same size as canvas to provide a firm stitching base.

To mark center of design on shirt, fold shirt in half lengthwise. Measure along folded edge desired number of inches from neck to center of design; mark with a pin.

Match center of canvas to pin on shirt; with canvas threads straight, pin canvas to shirt. Pin interfacing to wrong side of shirt. Baste thicknesses together.

Using a sharp needle, work design, stitching from large holes to large holes.

Trim canvas to within ½" of design. Dampen canvas until it becomes limp. Pull out canvas threads one at a time using tweezers.

Trim interfacing close to design.

Designs by Lorraine Birmingham.

A special friend will love this sentimental sweatshirt. With hugs and smiles, these bear buddies remind us of the warm feeling that comes when you open your heart to others.

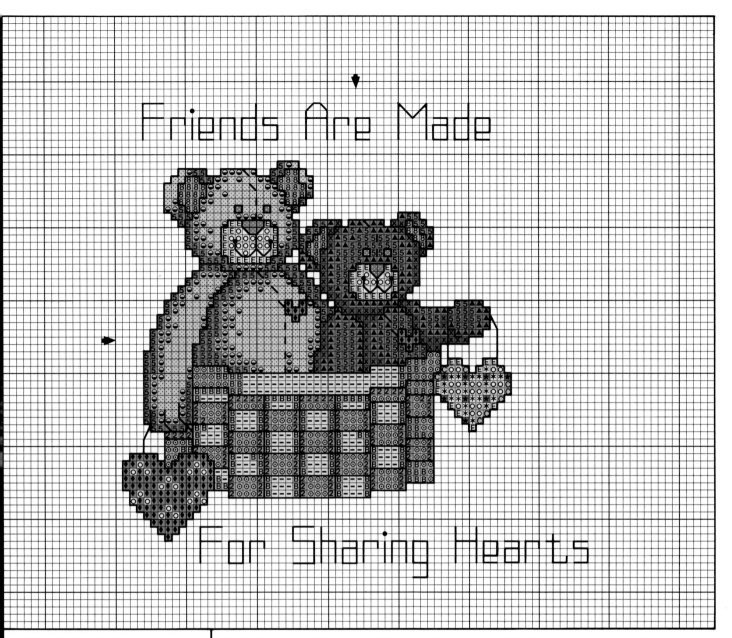

Friends Are Made

For Sharing Hearts

SHARING HEARTS (66w x 65h)				
X	DMC	¼X	B'ST	JPC	COLOR
O	ecru	☐		1002	ecru
▦	310	◣	╱	8403	black
◆	347			3013	red
2	420			5374	vy dk gold
✳	433			5471	lt brown
▲	434			5000	vy lt brown
5	435			5371	dk tan
◉	436			5943	tan
▨	437			5942	lt tan
▬	676			2874	lt gold
◎	680			2876	dk gold
B	729			2875	gold
E	739			5369	cream
8	801			5475	brown
✱	930		╱	7052	dk blue
C	931			7051	blue
✳	932			7050	lt blue
●	310	black French Knot			

Sharing Hearts was stitched over a 12" square of waste canvas (8.5 ct) on a purchased sweatshirt. Six strands of floss were used for Cross Stitch and 2 for all other stitches.

WORKING ON WASTE CANVAS

Waste canvas is a special canvas that provides an evenweave grid for placing stitches on fabric. After the design is worked over the canvas, the canvas threads are removed, leaving the design on the fabric. The canvas is available in several mesh sizes.

1. Cover edges of canvas with masking tape. Cut a piece of lightweight, non-fusible interfacing the same size as canvas to provide a firm stitching base.

2. To mark center of design on shirt, fold shirt in half lengthwise. Measure along folded edge desired number of inches from neck to center of design; mark with a pin.

3. Match center of canvas to pin on shirt. Use the blue threads in canvas to place canvas straight on shirt; pin canvas to shirt. Pin interfacing to wrong side of shirt. Baste all three thicknesses together as shown in **Fig. 1**.

4. Place design area in a screw-type hoop. We recommend a hoop that is large enough to encircle entire design. Roll excess fabric, including back of shirt, over top edge of hoop; pin in place.

5. Using a #24 tapestry needle, work design, stitching from large holes to large holes.

6. Trim canvas to within ¾" of design. Dampen canvas until it becomes limp. Pull out canvas threads one at a time using tweezers (**Fig. 2**).

7. Trim interfacing close to design.

Designed by Kathie Rueger.

Fig. 1

Fig. 2

GREATEST KID ON EARTH

CIRCUS ANIMAL MIX

- 12 cups popped popcorn
- 1 cup firmly packed brown sugar
- ½ cup butter or margarine
- ¼ cup dark corn syrup
- ¼ teaspoon salt
- ½ teaspoon baking soda
- 1 teaspoon vanilla extract
- 1 package (9 ounces) animal crackers (about 4 cups)
- 1 package (16 ounces) candy-coated chocolate-covered peanuts
- 1 package (7⅜ ounces) candy corn

Preheat oven to 200 degrees. Place popcorn in a large heat-resistant bowl. Butter the sides of a heavy medium saucepan. Combine brown sugar, butter, corn syrup, and salt in saucepan. Stirring constantly, cook over medium heat until sugar dissolves. Continuing to stir, bring syrup to a boil. Cook, without stirring, 5 minutes. Remove from heat. Stir in baking soda (syrup will foam) and vanilla. Pour syrup over popcorn, stirring until well coated. Spoon mixture into 2 greased 9 x 13-inch baking pans. Bake 1 hour, stirring every 15 minutes. Cool completely in pans. Stir in animal crackers and candies. Store in an airtight container.
Yield: about 22 cups snack mix

Youngsters will jump through hoops for this colorful tee, and a yummy batch of our sweet Circus Animal Mix is sure to make them roar with delight!

X	DMC	¼X	B'ST	ANC.	COLOR
▨	blanc	▨		2	white
◯	310	◢	╱	403	black
+	321			9046	red
✕	740			316	orange
◇	742			303	lt orange
✳	744			301	yellow

The design was stitched over a 12" square of 8.5 mesh waste canvas on a purchased T-shirt. Six strands of floss were used for Cross Stitch and 2 for Backstitch. See Working on Waste Canvas, page 143.

Design by Ferrie Lee Steinmeyer.
© 1996

73w x 55h

FOR A LITTLE ANGEL

This cute sweatshirt makes a heavenly gift for a little girl who's always a little angel in Sunday School. The thoughtful present is sure to make her shine all year!

SUNDAY SCHOOL SUNBEAM (42w x 52h)

X	DMC	¼X	B'ST	JPC	COLOR	X	DMC	B'ST	JPC	COLOR
	blanc			1001	white	V	761		3068	lt pink
	310		╱	8403	black	★	797		7023	blue
⊖	321	◨		3500	lt red	2	798		7022	lt blue
8	648			8390	grey	S	814		3044	dk red
3	743			2302	yellow	✳	816	╱	3410	red
O	744			2293	lt yellow	−	3072		6005	lt grey
+	754			2331	lt flesh	⊙	3378			dk flesh
▲	758			3868	flesh	●	blanc		white French Knot	
★	760			3069	pink	●	433		Indicates hair placement.	

Sunday School Sunbeam: Stitched over a 7" x 8" piece of 8.5 mesh waste canvas on a purchased child's sweatshirt. Six strands of floss used for Cross Stitch and 2 for all other stitches.

For each strand of hair, thread needle with a 6" length of six-strand brown floss. Insert needle from right to wrong side of shirt leaving 3" of floss on right side; insert needle back through to right side of shirt close to entry point. Remove needle and tie ends of floss in a double knot close to shirt; trim ends to ¼" from knot.

Working on Waste Canvas: Waste canvas is a special canvas that provides an evenweave grid for placing stitches on fabric. After the design is worked over the canvas, the canvas threads are removed, leaving the design on the fabric. The canvas is available in several mesh sizes.

1. Cover edges of canvas with masking tape. When working on lightweight fabric, cut a piece of lightweight, non-fusible interfacing the same size as canvas to provide a firm stitching base.

2. To mark center of design on shirt, fold shirt in half lengthwise. Measure along folded edge desired number of inches from top of shirt to center of design; mark with a pin.

3. Match center of canvas to pin on shirt. Use the blue threads in canvas to place canvas straight on shirt; pin canvas to shirt. Pin interfacing to wrong side of shirt. Baste all three thicknesses together.

4. Using a sharp needle, work design, stitching from large holes to large holes.

5. Trim canvas to within ¾" of design. Dampen canvas until it becomes limp. Pull out canvas threads one at a time using tweezers.

6. Trim interfacing close to design.

Designed by Joy Aldridge.

It's easy to turn plain chambray shirts into Western wear with our colorful cross stitch designs. Accented with red seed beads, the small mosaic motifs are perfect for embellishing yokes, collars, pockets, and plackets.

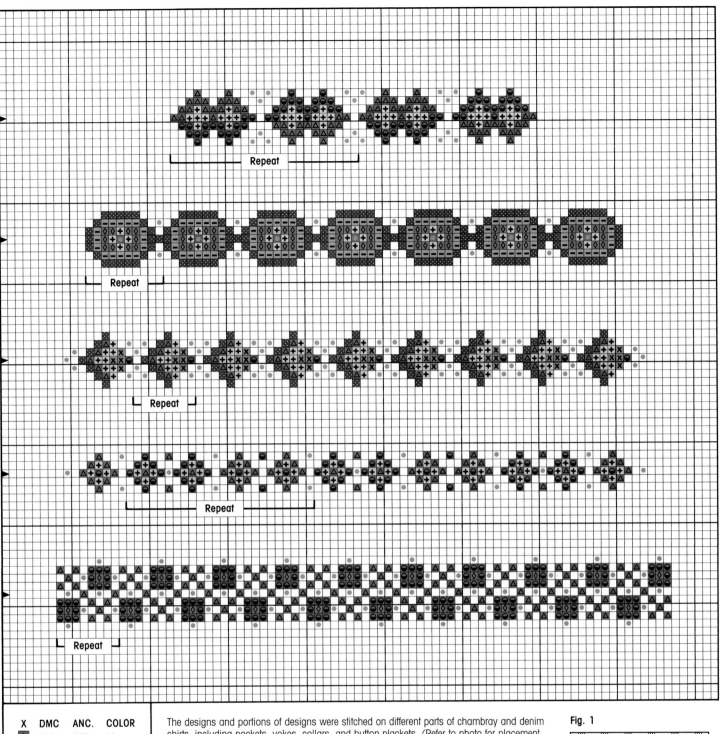

Repeat

Repeat

Repeat

Repeat

Repeat

The designs and portions of designs were stitched on different parts of chambray and denim shirts, including pockets, yokes, collars, and button plackets. (Refer to photo for placement suggestions.) The designs were worked over 8.5, 10, or 12 mesh waste canvas. Six strands of floss were used for Cross Stitch on 8.5 and 10 mesh waste canvas. Four strands of floss were used for Cross Stitch on 12 mesh waste canvas. See Working on Waste Canvas, page 143.

To sew beads in place use 2 strands of floss and a #8 sharp needle. Bring needle up at 1 (and all odd numbers); then run needle through bead and go down at 2 (and all even numbers) as shown in **Fig. 1**. Secure thread on back or move to next bead.

Designs by Barbara Baatz.

Fig. 1

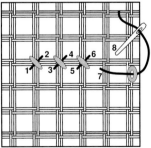

SHIPSHAPE SHIRTS

Our flags say it all! Patterned after the international flag code that ships use to signal each other, the colorful alphabet can be used to spell out names, phrases, and more. Whether stitched for seasoned sailors or contented landlubbers, the nautical sweatshirts are sure to make a big splash!

ALPHABET FLAGS (12w x 12h each)

X	DMC	JPC	COLOR
	blanc	1001	white
★	310	8403	black
C	312	7979	blue
-	725	2298	yellow
✳	817	2335	red

Adult Sweatshirts: Alphabet Flags stitched with three squares between each flag over 8.5 mesh waste canvas on adult-size sweatshirts. (See Working on Waste Canvas, page 143.) Six strands of floss used for Cross Stitch.

Child Sweatshirts: Alphabet Flags stitched with three squares between each flag over 10 mesh waste canvas on child-size sweatshirts. (See Working on Waste Canvas, page 143.) Five strands of floss used for Cross Stitch.

Designs by Nancy Spruance.

WINTER WARMERS

Use these cute designs to turn plain sweatshirts into enchanting winter wear for little boys and girls. Featuring woodland deer and toasty mittens, these adorable pullovers are just the thing for a chilly day.

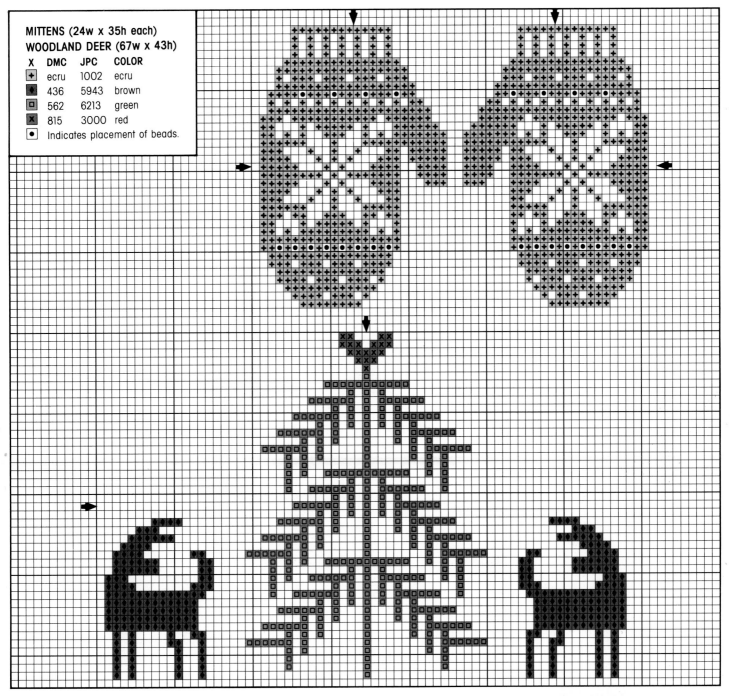

MITTENS (24w x 35h each)
WOODLAND DEER (67w x 43h)

X	DMC	JPC	COLOR
⊞	ecru	1002	ecru
◆	436	5943	brown
□	562	6213	green
✕	815	3000	red
•	Indicates placement of beads.		

Mittens: Each mitten stitched over a separate 4" x 6" piece of waste canvas (10 ct) on a purchased sweatshirt. Six strands of floss used for Cross Stitch. Referring to photo for placement, tack two lengths of ⅛"w ribbon to shirt at top of mittens and at neckband. Tie ribbon in a bow; trim ends. Sew red seed beads to mittens as indicated by chart.

Woodland Deer: Stitched over a 10" x 8" piece of waste canvas (10 ct) on a purchased sweatshirt. Six strands of floss used for Cross Stitch.

Working on Waste Canvas: Waste canvas is a special canvas that provides an evenweave grid for placing stitches on fabric. After the design is worked over the canvas, the canvas threads are removed, leaving the design on the fabric. The canvas is available in several mesh sizes.

1. Cover edges of canvas with masking tape. When working on lightweight fabric, cut a piece of lightweight, non-fusible interfacing the same size as canvas to provide a firm stitching base.

2. (Note: Waste canvas pieces for Mittens were turned at different angles on shirt; refer to photo for placement of designs.) To mark center of design on shirt, fold shirt in half lengthwise. Measure along folded edge desired number of inches from top of shirt to center of design; mark with a pin.

3. Match center of canvas to pin on shirt. Use the blue threads in canvas to place canvas straight on shirt; pin canvas to shirt. Pin interfacing to wrong side of shirt. Baste all three thicknesses together as shown in **Fig. 1**.

4. Using a sharp needle, work design, stitching from large holes to large holes.

5. Trim canvas to within ¾" of design. Dampen canvas until it becomes limp. Pull out canvas threads one at a time using tweezers (**Fig. 2**).

6. Trim interfacing close to design.

Designed by Polly Carbonari.

Fig. 1

Fig. 2

139

With these pretty bouquets, your pockets need never be empty. We stitched both of the designs on chambray shirts for year-round enjoyment.

POCKET BOUQUETS

X	DMC	1/4X	B'ST	JPC	COLOR	X	DMC	1/4X	B'ST	JPC	COLOR	X	DMC	1/4X	B'ST	JPC	COLOR
▒	blanc			1001	white	□	554			4104	lt purple	S	987	◪	◪	6258	green
△	307			2290	yellow	-	745			2296	lt yellow	X	3347		◪	6266	lt green
◉	309			3284	lt red	▲	815			3000	dk red	▒	3348		▫	6266	vy lt green
	310		◪	8403	black	◆	822			5830	beige	S	3716				lt pink
★	326			3401	red		890		◪	6021	vy dk green	X	3731				dk pink
+	335			3283	vy lt red	V	948			2331	peach	◇	3733				pink
◔	552			4092	dk purple	☆	963			3280	vy lt pink	●	blanc				white French Knot
C	553			4097	purple	▲	986		◪	6021	dk green	●	987				green French Knot

Each **Pocket Bouquet** design was stitched over a 10" x 8" piece of 11 mesh waste canvas on a purchased shirt with a 4¼" wide pocket opening. Four strands of floss were used for Cross Stitch, 2 for Backstitch and 3 for French Knots. Center design over pocket with the bottom row of stitching underneath the opening of the pocket.

Designed by Sandi Gore Evans.

Working on Waste Canvas: Waste canvas is a special canvas that provides an evenweave grid for placing stitches on fabric. After the design is worked over the canvas, the canvas threads are removed, leaving the design on the fabric. The canvas is available in several mesh sizes.
1. Cut two 2" slits in canvas as needed to slip canvas inside pocket (**Fig. 1**). Cut interfacing same size as canvas. To prevent raw edges of canvas from marring fabric, cover edges of canvas with masking tape.

Fig. 1

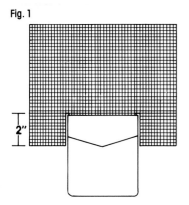

2. With canvas inside pocket, use the blue threads in canvas to place canvas straight along top edge of pocket; pin canvas to shirt. Pin interfacing to wrong side of shirt. To prevent canvas from slipping, baste securely around edge of canvas through all three thicknesses. Then baste from corner to corner and from side to side.
3. Place shirt in a hoop. The hoop helps keep the area not being stitched out of the way. Roll excess fabric over edge of hoop and pin in place.
4. Using a sharp needle, work design, stitching from large holes to large holes. Work design from bottom to top, placing bottom row of stitches underneath top edge of pocket.
5. Trim canvas to within ¾" of design. Use a sponge or spray bottle of water to dampen canvas until it becomes limp. Pull out canvas threads one at a time using tweezers.
6. Trim interfacing close to design.

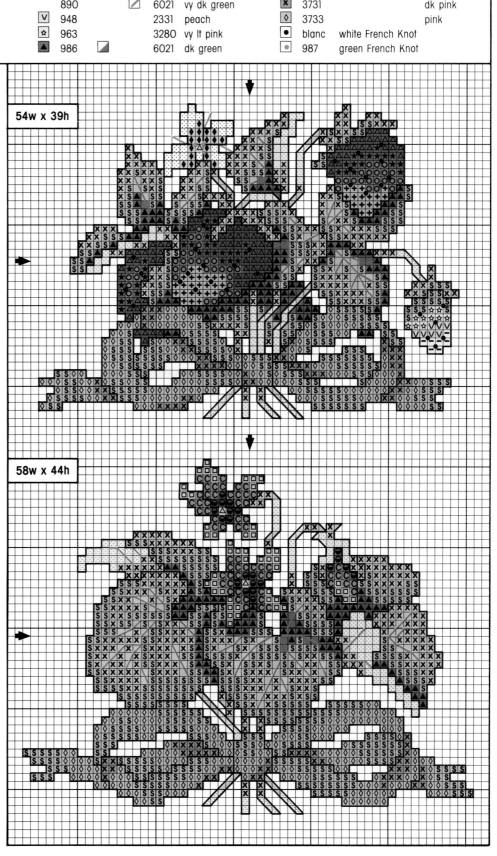

54w x 39h

58w x 44h

GENERAL INSTRUCTIONS
WORKING WITH CHARTS

How to Read Charts: Each of the designs is shown in chart form. Each colored square on the chart represents one Cross Stitch or one Half Cross Stitch. Each colored triangle on the chart represents one One-Quarter Stitch or one Three-Quarter Stitch. Black or colored dots represent French Knots. Black or colored ovals represent Lazy Daisy Stitches. The straight lines on the chart indicate Backstitch. When a French Knot, Lazy Daisy Stitch, or Backstitch covers a square, the symbol is omitted or reduced and placed on both sides of the French Knot, Lazy Daisy Stitch, or Backstitch.

Each chart is accompanied by a color key. This key indicates the color of floss to use for each stitch on the chart. The headings on the color key are for Cross Stitch (**X**), DMC color number (**DMC**), One-Quarter Stitch (**¼X**), Three-Quarter Stitch (**¾X**), Half Cross Stitch (**½X**), Backstitch (**B'ST**), J. & P. Coats color number (**JPC**), Anchor color number (**ANC.**), and color name (**COLOR**). Color key columns should be read vertically and horizontally to determine type of stitch and floss color.

How to Determine Finished Size: The finished size of your design will depend on the thread count per inch of the fabric being used. To determine the finished size of the design on different fabrics, divide the number of squares (stitches) in the width of the charted design by the thread count of the fabric. For example, a charted design with a width of 80 squares worked on 14 count Aida will yield a design 5¾" wide. Repeat for the number of squares (stitches) in the height of the charted design. (**Note:** To work over two fabric threads, divide the number of squares by one-half the thread count.) Then add the amount of background you want plus a generous amount for finishing.

STITCH DIAGRAMS

Counted Cross Stitch (X): Work a Cross Stitch to correspond to each colored square on the chart. For horizontal rows, work stitches in two journeys (**Fig. 1**). For vertical rows, complete each stitch as shown (**Fig. 2**). When working over two fabric threads, work Cross Stitch as shown in **Fig. 3**. When the chart shows a Backstitch crossing a colored square (**Fig. 4**), a Cross Stitch should be worked first; then the Backstitch (**Fig. 9 or 10**) should be worked on top of the Cross Stitch.

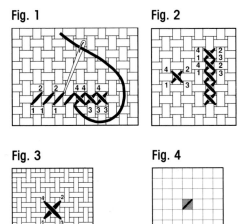

Fig. 1   Fig. 2

Fig. 3   Fig. 4

Quarter Stitch (¼X and ¾X): Quarter Stitches are denoted by triangular shapes of color on the chart and on the color key. Come up at 1 (**Fig. 5**); then split fabric thread to go down at 2. When stitches 1-4 are worked in the same color, the resulting stitch is called a Three-Quarter Stitch (**¾X**). **Fig. 6** shows the technique for Quarter Stitches when working over 2 fabric threads.

Fig. 5   Fig. 6

Half Cross Stitch (½X): This stitch is one journey of the Cross Stitch and is worked from lower left to upper right as shown in **Fig. 7**. When working over two fabric threads, work Half Cross Stitch as shown in **Fig. 8**.

Fig. 7   Fig. 8

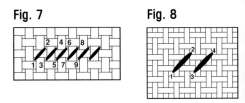

Backstitch (B'ST): For outline detail, Backstitch (shown on chart and on color key by black or colored straight lines) should be worked after the design has been completed (**Fig. 9**). When working over two fabric threads, work Backstitch as shown in **Fig. 10**.

Fig. 9   Fig. 10

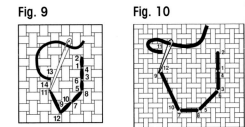

French Knot: Bring needle up at 1. Wrap floss once around needle and insert needle at 2, holding end of floss with non-stitching fingers (**Fig. 11**). Tighten knot; then pull needle through fabric, holding floss until it must be released. For larger knot, use more strands; wrap only once.

Fig. 11

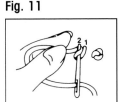

Lazy Daisy Stitch: Bring needle up at 1 and make a loop. Go down at 1 and come up at 2, keeping floss below point of needle (**Fig. 12**). Pull needle through and go down at 2 to anchor loop, completing stitch. (**Note:** To support stitches, it may be helpful to go down in edge of next fabric thread when anchoring loop.)

Fig. 12

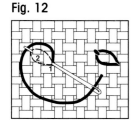

STITCHING TIPS

Working over Two Fabric Threads: Use the sewing method instead of the stab method when working over two fabric threads. To use the sewing method, keep your stitching hand on the right side of the fabric (instead of stabbing the fabric with the needle and taking your stitching hand to the back of the fabric to pick up the needle). With the sewing method, you take the needle down and up with one stroke instead of two. To add support to stitches, it is important that the first Cross Stitch is placed on the fabric with stitch 1-2 beginning and ending where a vertical fabric thread crosses over a horizontal fabric thread (**Fig. 13**). When the first stitch is in the correct position, the entire design will be placed properly, with vertical fabric threads supporting each stitch.

Fig. 13

Working on Waste Canvas: Waste canvas is a special canvas that provides an evenweave grid for placing stitches on fabric. After the design is worked over the canvas, the canvas threads are removed, leaving the design on the fabric. Most canvas has blue parallel threads every fifth square to aid in counting and in placing the canvas straight on the fabric. The blue threads may be placed horizontally or

vertically. The canvas is available in several mesh sizes. Use lightweight, nonfusible interfacing on wrong side of fabric to give a firmer stitching base. We recommend a screw-type hoop that is large enough to encircle entire design. Use a #24 tapestry needle for knit fabric. Use a sharp embroidery needle for tightly knit or tightly woven fabric. To ensure smoother stitches, separate strands and realign them before threading needle.

Step 1. Cut waste canvas 2" larger than design size on all sides. Cut interfacing same size as canvas. To prevent raw edges of canvas from marring fabric, cover edges of canvas with masking tape.

Step 2. Find desired placement for design; mark center of design on garment with a pin.

Step 3. Match center of canvas to pin. Use the blue threads in canvas to place canvas straight on garment; pin canvas to garment. Pin interfacing to wrong side of garment. To prevent canvas from slipping, especially on large designs, baste securely around edge of canvas through all three thicknesses. Then baste from corner to corner and from side to side as shown in **Fig. 14.**

Fig. 14

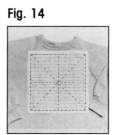

Step 4. Place garment in hoop. The hoop helps keep the area not being stitched out of the way. Roll excess fabric, including back of garment, over top edge of hoop and pin in place (**Fig. 15**).

Fig. 15

Step 5. Work design following Stitch Diagrams.

Step 6. Trim canvas to within ³/₄" of design. Use a sponge or spray bottle of water to dampen canvas until it becomes limp. Using tweezers, pull out canvas threads one at a time (**Fig. 16**).

Fig. 16

Step 7. Trim interfacing close to design.

FINISHING TECHNIQUES

Reversible Cross Stitch: (**Note:** Bring threaded needle up at **1** and all **odd** numbers and down at **2** and all **even** numbers. Dashed lines represent stitches on back.) For horizontal rows, work stitches in four journeys as shown in **Figs. 17 & 18**. For vertical rows, begin at the bottom and work stitches in four journeys as shown in **Figs. 19 & 20**. Stitch 25-26 in **Figs. 18 & 20** is used to carry floss to back. Secure end of floss by carefully weaving under a few stitches.

Fig. 17   **Fig. 18**

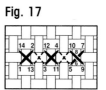

Fig. 19   **Fig. 20**

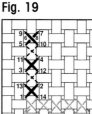
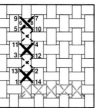

143

ROMANTIC MONOGRAMS

Continued from page 33.

Heart-Shaped Sachet

For lace ruffle, cut one 11" length of $1/2$"w pregathered lace. Matching edges and beginning at top of stitched piece, use a $1/4$" seam allowance to sew lace to right side of stitched piece.

With right sides facing and matching raw edges, pin stitched piece and backing fabric together. Using a $1/4$" seam allowance and leaving an opening for turning, sew pieces together. Clip seam allowance at curves and corners and turn heart right side out. Stuff heart with polyester fiberfill. Place a few drops of scented oil on a small amount of polyester fiberfill and insert in middle of sachet. Sew final closure by hand.

Jar Lid

The letter "P" was stitched on a 4" square of linen. It was inserted in the lid of a $2 3/4$" dia. porcelain jar.

Sachet Bag

The letter "R" was stitched on a 5" x $7 1/2$" piece of linen. For bag, center and stitch letter with the bottom $1 1/2$" from one short edge of the fabric. For backing, cut a second 5" x $7 1/2$" piece of same fabric as stitched piece. Fold a 24" length of $1/8$"w ribbon in half. On right side of stitched piece 2" from top, pin folded edge of ribbon even with left raw edge. With right sides facing and leaving top edge open, sew stitched piece and backing fabric together along sides and bottom using $1/2$" seam allowance. Trim corner seam allowances diagonally. Fold top edge of bag $1/4$" to wrong side; press. Fold $1/4$" again; hem. Sew desired pregathered lace trim to top edge and turn right side out. Stuff with polyester fiberfill. Place a few drops of scented oil on a small amount of polyester fiberfill and insert in middle of sachet. Tie ribbon in bow.

Square Sachet

The letter "A" was stitched on a 5" square of linen. For sachet, cut backing fabric same size as stitched piece. With finished edge toward center of sachet and gathered edge $3/4$" from design on all sides, baste desired pregathered lace trim to right side of stitched piece. With right sides facing and leaving an opening for turning, sew stitched piece and backing fabric together on basting line. Trim seam allowance to $1/4$" and turn right side out. Stuff with polyester fiberfill. Place a few drops of scented oil on a small amount of polyester fiberfill and insert in middle of sachet. Sew final closure by hand.

Towel

The letters "D", "K", and "B" were stitched on a 12" x 20" piece of linen. For towel, center and stitch letters 2 squares apart with the bottom of letters $2 1/2$" from one short edge. Fold each edge $1/4$" to wrong side; press. Fold $1/4$" again; hem. Sew desired pregathered lace trim to bottom edge of towel.

PANTRY SCARF FINISHING

Continued from page 115.

Measure depth of shelf and add 1". Referring to **Fig. 21**, cut bread cover determined measurement from top of design. Press cut edge $1/4$" to wrong side. Press $1/4$" to wrong side again and sew along pressed edge. Place scarf on shelf with sewn edge close to wall.

Fig. 21

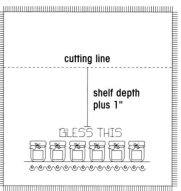

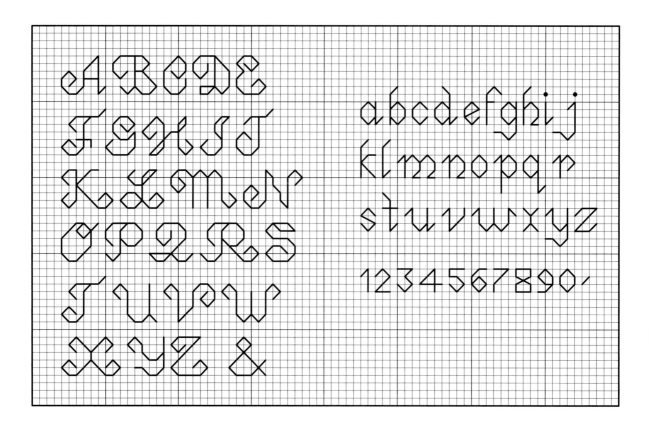

144